PRAIS

You Are Not Them is a timeless book of entrepreneurial wisdom... a must-read for both seasoned and starting entrepreneurs who are serious about success.

> **Marshall Goldsmith** | Thinkers 50 #1 Executive Coach and only two-time #1 Leadership Thinker in the world; New York Times #1 bestselling author of *Triggers*, and *Mojo*, and *What Got You Here Won't Get You There*.

In *You Are Not Them*, Sid Mohasseb—one of California's leading angel investors and business mentors—has written a lyrical, metaphysical paean to the entrepreneurial spirit that will serve as a poetic guidebook to self-actualization through business for a new generation of founders.

> **David S. Rose** | Founder, New York Angels; Executive Chairman of Gust

The right book at the right time! This book is a work of art for any entrepreneur who is misunderstood or realizes they were put on this planet for a reason, but need the encouragement to go, and as we say at Draper University, "Fail and Fail again until you Succeed!"

> **Tim Draper** | founder, Draper Fisher Jurvetson

Informative, unique, motivating. In his book, *You Are Not Them*, Sid Mohasseb sets you up for a real poetic journey of entrepreneurial self-exploration and leads you to re-examine your entrepreneurial uniqueness. If you're struggling to remember your own personal "why" or simply are overdue for some self-reflection, this is a must-read!

> **Laura Huang** | Professor, Harvard Business School; Author of international bestseller *Edge: Turning Adversity into Advantage*

A delightful combination of philosophy, poetry, great stories, and effective advice from an expert entrepreneur and investor. Sid Mohasseb surprises you and creates a canvas for you to see yourself as successful and satisfied in your entrepreneurism journey.

Dave Berkus | Super Angel, Chairman-Emeritus, the Tech Coast Angels; US Early-Stage Venture Capitalist of the Year

Highly motivating! Sid Mohasseb approaches entrepreneurship the way Socrates might have approached a complex theological question, or Michelangelo the Sistine Chapel — with utter respect and attention to detail. A refreshing perspective on business as both an art form and a way of life.

Shahin Farshchi | Partner, LUX Capital

A book that does not describe the entrepreneur as much as it captures the essence of what it is to be an entrepreneur. The use of quotations is particularly skillful and illuminating. They are like broken shards that refract and reflect the author's ideas in unexpected directions

Scott Siegler | Former President of Columbia Pictures and media investor

Like philosophy, entrepreneurship is not something you do, it is something you embody. This is not a 'how-to' book but rather one that helps entrepreneurs understand the spiritual essence of being. A Zen approach to life and business.

Bambi Francisco Roizen | Author of *Unequally Yoked*; Founder, Vator

To navigate risk is an inherent component of any entrepreneurial venture, but with what grace and courage you face that adversity is completely unique to the individual. You Are Not Them was an exploration into what makes an entrepreneur such a powerful and global catalyst for change. I finished this book with the feeling that everything I wanted to accomplish was just on the other side of my own limiting beliefs.

Kevin L. Jackson | CEO, GC GlobalNet; bestselling author of *Click to Transform*

You Are Not Them! was like spiritual comfort food! Instead of simply detailing a 12-step plan to financial freedom, Mohasseb draws on the wisdom of the world's greatest thinkers, philosophers, and poets to weave a powerful tapestry of inspiration and authenticity. I couldn't put it down.

Rick Orford | co-founder & executive producer, Travel Addicts Life; bestselling author of *The Financially Independent Millennial*

The concept of developing my own Personal Entrepreneurial Philosophy (PEP) was something completely foreign to me – and yet, I found the exercise incredibly rewarding. By defining my leadership values and identifying areas in which I was not actively living these moral imperatives, the path towards self-improvement became clear, actionable, and most importantly, effective.

Tamara Nall | President and CEO, Leading Niche

Entrepreneurship Philosophy does not pretend to be anything other than what it is – a collection of wisdom from some of the greatest minds in history. Mohasseb has penned a masterful narrative that will help you discover and transform the chinks in your mental armor.

Shawn Johal | Business Growth Coach; author of *The Happy Leader*

Sid Mohasseb approaches the idea of entrepreneurship as a craftsman and a philosopher. He proposes that, by nature, we are all entrepreneurs and artists; our life is the masterwork, and our choices color the canvas. When you avoid risk you are no longer a purposeful artist, one must recognize change is the fiber of life, it is our friend. By connecting to and learning how to leverage the various attributes of your own entrepreneurial spirit, the path toward true authenticity and success becomes clear. A highly recommended and original work!

Tom Fedro | President & CEO, Paragon
Software Group Corporation;
bestselling author of *Next Level Selling*

More than just another how-to business book, You Are Not Them! reads like a treatise on the mindset of what it means to truly encompass and embody the spirit of innovative thinking. An excellent book to re-center, refocus and redefine all the important criteria in your life.

Mark Nureddine | CEO, Bull Outdoor Products;
bestselling author of *Pocket Mentor*

Sid may be a very successful entrepreneur but he is definitely a high octane philosopher. This is not a "how-to" but much more interestingly perhaps... a why and where to start... I have always said *'perfection is overrated.'* But Sid says *"When perfection is constant, progress is meaningless, hope is vain, and life is pointless."* Which is way deeper than my little quip. And then he gives a thought path to back it up and weaves in messages from a long list of well-known philosophers, historians, authors, and more!! A great book for my shelf to be read and savored often.

Dennis Andrews | CEO, Scar Tissue;
bestselling author of *Too Blue!*

You Are Not Them truly captures the essence of an entrepreneurial journey and of the entrepreneurial mindset. As one who has been down this road many times himself, Sid Mohasseb knows and understands that an entrepreneurial journey starts with a simple question of "why" that reveals paths to delivering customer value.

Steven Mednick / Associate Professor of Clinical Entrepreneurship, Lloyd Greif Center for Entrepreneurial Studies, Marshall School of Business, University of Southern California

Sid Mohasseb reveals and guides the reader through a lyrical and spiritual journey about what it means to evolve as an entrepreneur. He shows there is no single blueprint for a successful entrepreneur, but rather each entrepreneur is unique and each aspiring entrepreneur needs to embed this essence into a fluid path forward while being authentic to one's self."-

John Harbison / Chairman-Emeritus of Tech Coast Angels

YOU ARE NOT THEM

The Authentic Entrepreneur's Way

Sid Mohasseb

Leaders
Press

AnaBasis

Moving The Base UP!

All poems within this text, unless otherwise cited,
are written by Sid Mohasseb.

ISBN 978-1-63735-050-8 (special ed.)
ISBN 978-1-63735-048-5 (pbk)
ISBN 978-1-63735-049-2 (ebook)

Library of Congress Control Number: 2020925593

To You with immense gratitude...

To those who have loved me for a single minute or a lifetime, my everlasting gratitude. Without you, I would not be. To those who showed me hatred and darkness, my most sincere thanks. Without you, my mortality had no boundaries.

To those who offered me a brief opportunity to look into their souls as we stood on a street corner, in an elevator, or across a teller window, thank you for sharing. To those children who showed me the joy of learning and the elderly who alerted me of the consequences of fear of death, I offer no less than a safe place in my heart.

To those who showed me compassion by their simple, pure, and sincere commitment to the needy, I thank you for not submitting to reality. To those who showed me greed, and those who helped me unmask my ego, my hat is off to you for exposing the pitfalls of being human.

To those giants of philosophy and literature who offered their perspective without fear of judgment and to every individual in every town and every studio who has ever offered his or her version of beauty and sadness, I pledge an ocean of appreciation. Without you, the rounded edges of my illusions would have been rough and without soul.

And, my everlasting gratitude to all travelers who shared the path with me and all those who kept their distance and refused to derail my soul.

With immense gratitude, I dedicate this book to YOU.

DELEGATING AUTHORSHIP

> **Authors are expected to exert authority.**
>
> When it comes to authoring
> the story of your life,
> **you are the ONLY authority**
> and I am merely a provoker.

CONTENTS

FOREWORD

So, you think you want to be an entrepreneur. Or maybe you are an entrepreneur and you want to be a *better* entrepreneur.

Congratulations! You're looking at the right book. That's the good news. The less good news, as Sid Mohasseb will tell you early in this wonderful book, is that this is not a "how-to" manual. His premise, one that I strongly believe in, is that no two people are alike. Our genetic code provides for enough diversity that we can safely say that there are no exact twins among all the people who have ever lived and who will live in the foreseeable future (unless we figure out how to manufacture such twins by cloning, a future too bizarre to even think about).

The obvious conclusion is that we are different enough from each other that a detailed how-to plan that works for a single individual should not be expected to work for another. But Sid has a unique approach to creating better entrepreneurs. He believes that the attributes necessary for any human to become an entrepreneur are already within us.; they need only to be cultivated, shaped, and refined. It is that process that is developed, in an understandable and practical way in his book.

Sid suggests that you create a vision of yourself as a successful entrepreneur and offers you tools to aid you in executing that creation. He uses the metaphor

You are the sculptor
And
You are the sculpture!

You are the only person with enough knowledge of *you* to create a more refined *you*. He starts by defining the attributes of entrepreneurship and offers to take you on a journey that will provoke you to build your own entrepreneurial philosophy, one based upon your understanding of yourself. This will not be an easy journey. It will require the application of the concepts of mindfulness and of objectivity. But I predict that, if you stick it out, it will be an immensely productive journey.

Sid is too modest when he describes his ethos as the entrepreneurial philosophy. I predict that there will be more to this journey than entrepreneurship. You will find that life involves a series of entrepreneurial decisions and that the tools described in this book have the potential to change your entire life, not just the entrepreneurial part of it, for the better.

The journey itself will be a pleasant one because Sid, aside from his deep knowledge of business and creativity, is a humanist, and a poet. He enhances his wisdom with quotes from an eclectic group of philosophers from Jalâluddîn Rumi, 13th century poet and metaphysicist, to Mark Twain, from Lao Tzu, the Chinese philosopher, to Art Buchwald, from the Roman philosopher Seneca to Anais Nin and Gaugin.

I can't guarantee that Sid Mohasseb's book will make you a better entrepreneur or a better person, but I can guarantee that you will enjoy his poetry, his wisdom, and his logic. And you will rethink what life and business are all about.

Martin Cooper
December 2020

PART ONE: IN CONCLUSION

Every beginning is an end, and every end a new beginning!

"First lines did not define last pages in real life the way they did in books."
—Stephanie Butland,
The Lost for Words Bookshop

CHAPTER ONE:

THE SCULPTOR & THE SCULPTURE

You are the sculptor
and you are the sculpture!
Known and unknown,
shiny and dull,
always in flux,
always becoming;
never still, never static.
One minute here
the next, it's gone.
Always shaping and
then reshaping.
The sculpture that you chisel
with every choice
and every action.
That you may also
shape with your choice of
sameness and stagnation.
That is what you reap,
that is what you sow.

You are the sculpture,
the art that is
your imagination framed,
your soul exposed,
your hard work's earnings,
the child of your actions
and offspring of inactions.

Carved with your wisdom
you are the sculpture
that you create.
It is all that you are;
it is every mean
also, the end
and the promise
of all that you can be.
Cracked in some corners,
magnificent in others;
always in the making,
ready for repair.

As you whittle
you form the stone
and shape the clay.
The face without
and the content within:
the masterpiece you conceive.
The prospect you cast
holds all of your being; it reflects the past,
it holds the promise, the unwritten tale, of your future.

The sculpture is you,
a masterpiece in the making.
You are the clay; you are the stone;
you are the hammer and the chisel;
the oil that shines;
the soil that restores.
You are the color;
you are the brush.

**You are the artist,
the sculptor and the sculpture,
always in the making at every minute of every day.**

—Sid Mohasseb, author

--<>--

By nature, you are an entrepreneur and a sculptor. By choice, an authentic original, a pilot, an ocean, and a dancer. You are an artist who masterfully colors their entrepreneurial talent.

Your choices lay the stones of your path to tomorrow. They also shape the consequences and outcomes. Choose to be a purposeful sculptor. Realize that the boxes that limit your thoughts and actions are a figment of your imagination; a side effect of your inability to effectively tap into your inherent talents. To unleash the true power of your entrepreneurial genius, rise up. Unlearn the status quo and be an unwritten letter. A blank canvas to paint on; unformed clay ready to be shaped into a masterpiece. Position yourself to realize your stroke of genius: you are the sculpture of you. Always remember: you are not them!

The spirit of entrepreneurship is a life force for the purposeful sculptor. Embrace the spirit: hunt for knowledge in order to inspire action in exchange for often better, but uncertain, results. Acknowledge where you are positioned on the entrepreneurial spectrum; color your talents; seek to be awakened and aspire to become a practitioner and a forever apprentice. No matter where you start, you are always in transition – always in pursuit. Keep your eyes squarely on the exchange; the entrepreneurial trade of one situation for an improved one as you navigate risk.

Pursue your love of wisdom. The love that involves what you know and what you do. The wisdom that involves the realization that there is much you don't know and there are barriers to what you can do. The wisdom that expands as you act and as you learn. Your "philosophy" is the "love" (*philo* in Greek) you have for "wisdom" (*sophia*). To pursue, you have to be a philosopher – a lover of wisdom. Build and refine your unique philosophy which makes you the sculptor who creates a perpetually perfecting masterpiece. Shape and evolve your Personal Entrepreneurial Philosophy (PEP). Let it brighten the world you explore. Your love for wisdom, your philosophy, is shaped by your morality, priorities, view on creativity, leadership, inclusion, risk, and more. At best, what you pursue is what you achieve. Weave your love of wisdom into your decisions and in what you choose to be. Blend it with the clay and harmonize it with the stone of your sculpture. Color your talents and your sculpture over and over with the rainbow of your imagination.

Decide what "to be," not just once, but over and over. Continuously pave your unique path to the future. Recognize the importance of your ecosystem (your Ocean) and define your Oceanness. Your sculpture belongs to more than just you. It is a living entity that provides and connects; it is a force of movement and prosperity. Your choices are influenced by your ecosystem and the dimensions of your Oceanness.

As you chisel your sculpture, you risk damage. But when you aim to avoid risk, you are no longer a purposeful artist. Realize the constant need to navigate risk while embracing uncertainty like a pilot. You need to "wander" before reaching "Eureka." To explore is to risk. Accept the wisdom of evolution and appreciate probability – the reality of risk, odds, and outcomes. To accept risk is to acknowledge that there can be failure. Don't chase failure but nurse its wounds when it comes; the wounds of failure are the pathways to wisdom and the gateway to success. Embrace your world of beginnings and ends. A world of constant change – progression and regression.

Admit that every ending is a beginning and every beginning is an end. Every time you are at work, begin with a fresh perspective and end with an idea formed. Appreciate the critical impact of shifting in perspective, time, and shape. Learn to dance with both opportunities and the challenges of life and change. As a sculptor, you must view your art from every direction to find imperfections. To create perfection, you must be intimate with every curve and corner. You must realize the effect of time and shadows. To dance, pivot, and shift, is to find the right problems to solve, remain relevant, and execute by both discovering and sustaining advantages.

--<>--

"Some are cast in metal
others chipped from stone
yet more are shaped by hand in clay
what you sculpt, you own.

I yearned to feel the chisel
every scrape an evolution
each fetter of the holy rasp
my growing absolution.

I dream of you approaching
to polish me anew
so I may shine in constant thanks
at being made by you."

**—Excerpts from the Sculptor poem,
by Twenty-nine Pearls**

Any good cook knows that it's not just about following the recipe. Be the greatest by being the authentic YOU. Your sculpture is uniquely yours when you truly apply your talents and choose not to blindly follow "how-tos." As a sculptor, you know that what you created in the past is in the past and what lies ahead is a masterpiece still unformed. To shape your sculpture, you may use old clay or build on an old frame. Regardless, what you create is new. Your sculpture marries your origins and your originality. Appreciate the authentic you and your unique sculpture. But always remain under construction. Never finished but always evolving.

Be always in awe of what is ahead. Welcome the wanderlust you are born with. Let your purposeful wanderlust guide you towards your next best version – the sculpture of you that you can admire. Not because it is perfect, but because it is your evolving creation. Your love for wisdom is the philosophy that guides your wanderlust and your sense of discovery. Become intimate with your sculpture and the purpose it serves. Be aware of your "whys" and create to reveal them. As a purposeful sculptor, dive into the unknown to discover the new or the previously unseen. Your burning desire to always create, your wanderlust, is the spark that flames a thousand torches of creativity.

*"Keep your face always toward the sunshine
and shadows will fall behind you."*
—Walt Whitman, American journalist, father of free verse

Your thirst for wisdom activates your mindfulness. It feeds it and fuels your journey. It makes you mindful of the road ahead and its jagged paths. Mindful of both sides of crisis – opportunity and danger. Mindful of your judgement and your choices. Be mindful to learn and watch for teachers, people, and situations that are always around you. Use the energy of your nervousness to break your limits. Be mindful of vulnerabilities and of inherent powers – yours and others. Attach to ideas and actions with passion. But stand ready to detach and follow your journey.

Your actions actuate your mindfulness. Your actuated mindfulness shines a light on your sculpture from the outside in. It ignites the fires that can help you purify and improve your sculpture, over and over.

"Don't explain your philosophy. Embody it."
—Epictetus, Greek philosopher who was born a slave

Chisel away.
Express your genius;
because you deserve it.
Start today.

---<>---

The END & The BEGINNING

<<END OF PART ONE>>

Next, let's begin our journey **TO DISCOVER, IGNITE, AND EVOLVE** IN LIFE AND ENTREPRENEURSHIP.

But, **BEFORE WE BEGIN** to explore the _lay of the land_, there are _candid forewarnings_ and a _challenging appeal_.

PART TWO: DISCOVER & PURSUE

"Whether it's the best of times or the worst of times, it's the only time we've got."
—Art Buchwald, American humorist

It is TIME to DISCOVER and to PURSUE

CHAPTER TWO:

BEFORE WE BEGIN

The journey ahead is not about learning to think outside the box. It is about realizing that the boxes that limit our thoughts and actions are a figment of our imagination; a side effect of our inability to tap into our inherent talents. Your mental excursion does not end with a twelve-step process to follow, seven habits to embrace, or ten commandments to obey. It ends with a beginning: building your Personal Entrepreneurship Philosophy (PEP). Your PEP is an ever-evolving mental platform that will help you translate your wisdom into your choices, deeds, and consequences in entrepreneurship and in life.

My ambition is to help you find the cracks in your sameness and in the status quo of your thinking. My hope is that you will shape your unique composite of characteristics and release the power of your talents.

First, I aim to provoke you to discover or rediscover your talents and choose to explore them; whether you are a seasoned entrepreneur ready for new frontiers, a budding entrepreneur who is ready to blossom, or someone whose entrepreneurial talents have not yet been awakened. I want to unveil the connections between entrepreneurship and life in general and erase the myth of exclusivity of this magical and universal talent.

Next, I aspire for you to become your own provoker to shape and reshape the masterpiece that is you. To motivate is to provide a motive—a reason that causes a person to act in a certain way. When it comes to building your next best version, no one can cause you to evolve; no one holds the key to your future and no one can chart the course. Motivation may get you behind a canvas, it may place the brush in your hand, but it does not make you an artist. To be a painter, you must paint. To be a sculptor, you must chisel, mold and refine. To continue your evolution and shape your next best version, you must go beyond motivation. You must act and then provoke yourself to act again and again.

I hope this book ends with your new beginning. The choice is yours.

---<>---

THE CANDID FOREWARNING

STOP HERE if you are looking for a "How-To" book.

CONTINUE if you are ready for a mental voyage, an exploration within to form and reform the way you think. Continue if you are willing to make choices and write your own personal "how-tos." Join the journey if you are ready to evolve. Continue if you are willing to take responsibility for authoring your next chapter.

Neither life nor entrepreneurship come with a cookbook filled with generic recipes. "How-tos" are designed to provide you with step-by-step descriptions of how you can accomplish a task. But entrepreneurship is not a task – neither is life. Entrepreneurship begins with how you think and not what you do. It is a talent that can be awakened by your choices. Great entrepreneurs recognize that they are always apprentices and never masters. They adhere to William Shakespeare's thesis: "The fool doth think he is wise, but the wise man knows himself to be a fool." There are no maps for the journey of life or entrepreneurship and there are no shortcuts to success.

Any fool knows that he is unique and so is his path to greatness.

---<>---

THE CHALLENGING APPEAL

I appeal to you to retire your biases and addictions to the status quo. It is time to be a fallow field and an unwritten letter.

Skilled farmers know that a field has to be plowed before a new crop is seeded. They don't throw a bunch of seeds down and hope that they grow, either. Let your mind first be a fallow field. Then let your wisdom germinate the seeds and guide their growth. To get a good harvest, you must plow before seeding. Before you start the journey of shaping your PEP, let your mind be a fallow field, ready for new seeding and a new harvest.

I urge you to clear your mind. Be an unwritten letter; a blank cerebral page on which to write your story. Stay ready to examine and accept new perspectives. Some of the ideas ahead may appear novel and others nostalgic. Some definitions will fit the conventions you are accustomed to and others will be in conflict. Remain open to consider ideas equally before you discard them.

There are intended conflicts in arguments and rapid shifts in perspectives. Your objective is to reimagine not to reconfirm. You are the sculptor who is not bound by the past or conventions; create your next best version freely.

"Be an unwritten letter; a fallow field."
—Jalâluddîn Rumi, 13ᵗʰ century poet and metaphysicist

THE LAY OF THE LAND

Here is how our mental journey will unfold.

PART TWO: Discover & Pursue

Together, we will examine the role of change in life and entrepreneurship, as change is at the core of all choices and consequences. You will be faced with an alternative premise for entrepreneurship. A perspective rooted in your innate ability and talent to exchange one thing for another in order to prosper and improve. We will scan the entrepreneurial landscape and its dynamics - the colors, states, and triggers and reflect on various entrepreneurial modes. You will be encouraged to pursue your love of your wisdom and build your PEP.

PART THREE: Ignite & Be

Your genetic code of wanderlust will be explored and the jagged path we all face, regardless of origins, examined. The premise that you can be what you choose to "be" will be examined in light of various critical life and entrepreneurship dimensions: i) navigating risk like a pilot, ii) shaping your Oceanness, your ability to be a provider to your ecosystem, a connector with flexibility and a force to be feared, iii) being the authentic YOU and tapping into your axiom of choices, and iv) learning to act as a dancer and shifter as you experience victory and defeat and cross the last mile of execution and creation. IGNITE and BE, because to BE is the first step of becoming your superior self.

PART FOUR: Evolve & Become

Your talents are in full bloom as you actuate your mindfulness and begin to evolve. The world is a promising mess, unpredictable but filled with opportunities. As you shape and reshape your next best version, your sculpture, you will experience the wounds of failure and learn the art of nervousness. In your journey to become, you will cause and face many crises; you will be judged and will judge others. Before you begin again, you will rediscover and reenergize your entrepreneurial talent and sketch a new draft of your PEP.

PART FIVE: The Beginning

In the final chapter, you will begin your never-ending journey to evolve and become a mindful artist, a sculptor always at work, and an author with full authority.

---<>---

"On a day when the wind is perfect,
the sail just needs to open and the world is full of beauty.
Today is such a day."

—Jalâluddîn Rumi,
13th century poet and metaphysicist

---<>---

Let's begin,
Before you begin again!

First affirm a magical, unbreakable, and undeniable alliance: **A MARRIAGE MADE IN THE HEAVENS.**

CHAPTER THREE:

A MARRIAGE MADE
THE HEAVENS

It is spring. The world is filled with beautiful flowers in bright mesmerizing colors. The birds are chirping, all with perfect pitch and in harmony. The temperature is seventy-two degrees every day and spring showers are precisely timed – no surprises. All donuts are perfectly round and all people are fed. All leaders are just. All employees are one hundred percent productive and all students are summa cum laude.

The summer, fall, and winter ahead are all equally perfect. There are no killer hurricanes or viruses, no accidents on snowy days, no one is unjustly murdered, beaches are all sandy white and nights are filled with glittering stars. Death for everyone is predetermined and no one has a choice to fight back or recover from an illness. There are no variations or abnormalities. There are no changes or choices.

That is not only an unreal scenario of life, it is also an unreasonable and unacceptable existence. When perfection is constant, progress is meaningless, hope is vain, and life is pointless. If life stays permanently normal and a state of abnormal is demolished forever, the dark forces of stagnation will suffocate humanity and nature. Life as we know it ends. Life and evolution exist only if change exists. If there are no changes, no alternatives that require a decision and no choices to be made or actions to be taken, there is no life. The partnership between change and choice is eternal. It is this magnificent unbreakable marriage that leads to the birth of life itself, over and over. A marriage made in heaven from day one of the universe!

The sun rises and sets every day. But, since the beginning of time, no two days have been precisely the same. The sameness of repeatable groundhog days is only feasible in movies. Change is not an intrusion, it is the very fiber of life. Change drives your every breath. It is what makes the trees grow and what allows the sun to rise. Change is the bridge your children have to cross before they grow and prosper. Change makes normal tolerable and your choices hopeful. Change creates the choices that drive your decisions and actions. The very choices that influence who you are and who you can become in life and through entrepreneurship.

Change is NOT your enemy, It is the friend that keeps you alive.

---<>---

To see beyond the fog of sameness, to ascend above the horizon of the now and to escape the prison of normal, you must rise up from within. Rise up in order to realize that change is hidden in the essence of every minute of every day, concealed in every choice you face, every decision you make, and every consequence you experience. Rise up from within and gain access to your veiled talents; unlock the magical talent of entrepreneurship that turns you into an alchemist. The innate ability that makes you a transformer of ideas and resources into improved life situations: a sculptor.

When you realize the uniqueness of your choices, you realize that change does not apply to all people equally. The partnership of your choices and the changes you face or cause is also distinctive.

Don't look at every vagabond,
that you are exceptional to me.

You are still invisible,
have not seen your beauty.
One morning like a sun
you will rise from within

Tear down the cloud of your body,
as you are the stunning moon
hidden behind the fog.

You are a hawk
whose feet are chained.
With your own hand,
you must break the chain.

How joyous would it be,
when pure gold meets fire?
When it reveals its
art and talents.

Don't run away
from the flames of the fire
What would you lose if you try?

God be my witness,
you will not burn
because
you are born from gold.

—Jalâluddîn Rumi,
13th century poet and metaphysicist,
selected and translated text

Change is always ahead. Vast choices are also always ahead. Rise up to the challenge of change and choice. Maya Angelou claims, "You find the path by walking it." Rise up and walk your path with purpose. Discover the gold within, the potential for a better you- an improved you. To evolve and become witness to the marriage of choice and change you must believe that to leave the past behind and to step into the future will not harm you; believe that you will not burn, because you are born from gold.

---<>---

From day one, you were built to evolve and become.

The need to change is hidden in your wanderlust quality. Make your **WANDERLUST PURPOSEFUL** and expand your choices.

CHAPTER FOUR:

PURPOSEFUL WANDERLUST

**Your genetic wanderlust
provokes you to look for choices
when faced with change
and to make changes
to discover more choices!**

Your need to go, to move, to change, and to choose are hidden in the fabric of your genes. According to research from Texas A&M University, these genetic bits entered our DNA about 500,000 years ago, long before the human history of farming and hunting. The simple conclusion by researcher Dr. J. Timothy Lightfoot encapsulates the cause for this genetic mutation: "If you were lazy then, you did not survive."

Half a million years later, if you are lazy, you will not thrive and evolve, neither in business nor in life. You will stagnate. Your "wanderlust" is within your genes. A necessity that applies to your physical movement as well as mental transformation.

When you embrace and apply your wanderlust purposefully, you actively seek to fulfill your destiny. You partner with change and declare your clear intent, passion, and readiness to continually create the sculpture of you.

Everything begins within. Look inside to discover your inner wanderlust. Let your drive and desire stimulate you to purposefully choose and change. Let it guide you toward opportunities and situations to exchange one form of resource and ability with another, despite the risks involved. To make your wanderlust purposeful is to yearn to find your true nobility, "becoming superior to your former self," because there is nothing honorable about being superior to others. It is waking up, grinding, and getting better every day, as Sabrina Ionescu, a young and promising basketball player, learned from Kobe Bryant. Famously known as "Black Mamba," Kobe maintained a purposefully wanderlust until the last days of his short life. His drive to become the best in his craft as a basketball player made him a champion; but his lust to always wander, to learn and evolve as an investor, a filmmaker, and an author is what made him purposeful in his journey. His continual and focused curiosity positioned him as a visionary leader, a role model, and a hero for many. Kobe Bryant continued exploring and enhancing (coloring) his talents and shaped his path wherever he walked. He danced with change every chance he got.

Your wanderlust is purposeful when you make the journey *itself* the "why" you begin or the reason you restart and continue on your path. When you realize that nothing works forever and are not afraid to take the roads less traveled, you are expressing your wanderlust. When you believe that the more you purposefully wander, the more you discover; when you trust that the more you innovate, there will be even more opportunities to invent a purposeful you.

**Your wanderlust is
guided and deliberate
when you admit that
the more you create,
the more creativity you possess.**

Be always ready to attach to ideas, paths, and actions but also stay eager to detach, in the interest of new discoveries. Implode your addiction to sameness. Explode your choices and ignite your creativity. Tap into your wanderlust quality. Let it consume you. Work to maintain a desire to go even when the light at the end of the tunnel is not visible; look for your hidden genius, the artist within you.

In your journey, always remember that you are not in search of yourself, but in search of ways to reveal your authentic self. You are an artist, a sculptor. The impetus of your lust to wander is not only to survive but to thrive. It is to form, reform, and evolve the sculpture that is you.

---<>---

Next, and before you begin to color your entrepreneurial talent, master the **FRUITFUL EXCHANGE.**

CHAPTER FIVE:

THE FRUITFUL EXCHANGE

You are the fruit of
an entrepreneurial and life exchange!

I propose that entrepreneurship is a talent you possess. It is an ability that, if stimulated, guided, and unleashed, exposes you to the domain of ambiguity, the science of uncertainty, the art of innovation, and the power of choice. You are an entrepreneur whether you like it or not!

> *"We find comfort among those who agree with us
> – growth among those who don't."*
>
> **—Frank A. Clark, U.S. Congressman**

You must forget about the definition of entrepreneurship you have adopted so far. You have to unlearn the status quo and become an "unwritten letter." When you confine your abilities with words and preconceived definitions, you limit the vastness of your talents. Let your mind be unconstrained and explore the infinite dimensions of the galaxy offered by entrepreneurship. Remember the "challenging appeal:" Be an unwritten letter; a fallow field.

---<>---

Jean-Baptist Say, a French economist during the late 1700s, originally defined an entrepreneur as the individual who looks for inefficient uses of resources and capital and moves them into more productive, higher yield areas. According to Say, entrepreneurs must be able to recognize opportunities and manage them effectively. My mother, a homemaker, similarly looked for resources inefficiently used with an aim to put them to better use. Parents everywhere have been doing this for centuries! Isn't that also the role of every corporate manager?

Richard Cantillon, an Irish-French economist, is credited with the first use of the word entrepreneur as a "risk taker." This term referred to anyone who bought or made a product at a certain cost to sell at an uncertain price: risking resources against an unknown outcome. Every college student invests their time, many sleepless nights, and a lot of money, to gain knowledge and a degree. They wish to use that product to profit for the rest of their lives. Students are uncertain about the return on their investment and take a risk in innovating a new future for themselves. Under Cantillon's definition, all students are entrepreneurs!

Peter Drucker, the Austrian-born American management consultant, educator, and author, believed that the term "entrepreneur" should only apply to people who create something new and "people who change or transmute values." According to Drucker, the entrepreneur always searches for change, responds to it, and exploits it as an opportunity. You likely strive to create and seek advantages for yourself or your company? You also likely aim to exploit the opportunities available to you, both at home and at work. Entrepreneurship is not about results; it is about the process. Although sometimes unsuccessful, you likely search for value and aim to change your situation as needed. Using Drucker's definition, a sales representative at a clothing store faced with a slow sales day who moves (changes or transmutes value) the merchandise around the store in order to create a more welcoming display (shaping something new in search of economic value) is acting as an intrapreneur (someone who promotes an innovative strategy or idea within a company) or an entrepreneur who operates in a big corporate environment. With Drucker's definition, every action you take to create value and improve outcomes for yourself, your family, your employer, your own company, or your society is an act of entrepreneurship.

Some claim that the word entrepreneur is a combination of the two Latin words "entre," to undertake, and "prender," to understand and grasp. In other words, the person who sets out to "undertake the act of learning," is an entrepreneur – a definition that fits almost every intellectual and scientist. If you have ever learned anything, you have exercised entrepreneurship. Consider this: when you ask your kids to "go out there and learn something new," you are promoting entrepreneurship! You are stimulating the activation of their entrepreneurial talent! It remains their choice, however, to act on and embrace their talent in whatever way they desire.

Over time, the word "entrepreneur" has evolved into different meanings for different people. Today, some individuals label every person who works for themselves as an entrepreneur and some exclusively use the word when big dreams and big money are involved. Others brand every fast-talking individual who seeks to make a quick buck as an entrepreneur. In fact, the truth about the talent of "entrepreneurship" is hidden behind individual and theoretical impressions, perceptions, and labels.

What remains constant and applies across all definitions, however, is the spirit of entrepreneurship: seeking knowledge to stimulate doing something new by applying skills and creativity in exchange for an uncertain outcome that is anticipated to be better.

Which, I propose, is also the purpose of life!

---<>---

Entrepreneurship is not about money! It is about any uncertain exchange in pursuit of happiness.

When you take an online course to position yourself for a promotion or to change your career, you are acting in an entrepreneurial manner. You are looking at your options for the future, deciding to chart a specific path by taking the course, and despite an uncertain promotion or outcome, applying your creativity and skills and exchanging your time and money for a possibility. When you buy a gift for your spouse, you are exchanging your money and the time you spend to find the gift, for the happiness of someone else. You are applying your knowledge of what they like, along with creativity, to purchase a gift in exchange for happiness, both yours and theirs. You consider the outcome to have a higher value than your money and your time.

Entrepreneurship is not one state, but many. Entrepreneurs are not exact replicas with a common aim or one common path. Though entrepreneurial drive may be similar, each individual charts their own journey and the exchanges which ensue. Artists, farmers, janitors, philosophers, and scientists can all practice entrepreneurship; so can innovators, investors, bankers, clerks, and priests. Your entrepreneurial talent can shine in many different ways – it is not about beginnings and ends, but about the transformational state of mind and the actions you can take at any given time. Entrepreneurs constantly occupy different states and always look for a better way!

"There's a way to do it better – find it."
—Thomas A. Edison, American inventor and businessman

---<>---

Before pursuing your PEP, discover the **STATE** of entrepreneurship you occupy today and what can trigger a change. As you choose and change, you **COLOR** the rainbow of your entrepreneurship. You color your entrepreneurial talent and **TRIGGER** your evolution.

Your life is your coloring book. It's time to pick up the brush!

CHAPTER SIX:

COLORS, STATES, AND TRIGGERS

Imagine a body of clear, refreshing. pristine water sourced from the streams of the heavens. Now, picture your entrepreneurial talent: your pure and unencumbered talent that is ready to accept your color of choice. Your choices are the small drops of color you introduce into this untainted water. As you make choices in how to use your talents and who you are, your entrepreneurial talent becomes lightly colored. This is how you customize your talent and your art. As you color your talent, you choose or highlight a *state of entrepreneurship*. You always have a choice to add more colors; purple, yellow, red, or gray: colors inspired by the challenges you face, the environment you live in, your personality, your creativity, and your mindfulness. You can also neutralize colors, correct course, and refine the applications of your talent. Your amazing entrepreneurial talent can be displayed in infinite mesmerizing colors. The distinguishing colors reveal your uniqueness.

As you add more colors you choose a state of entrepreneurship: a condition of denial, aspiration, misguidedness, foolishness, or even exertion. The entrepreneurship galaxy includes a range of positions – mental planets which you can occupy; places you prefer psychologically, emotionally, and intellectually to travel to. Each reflects a state of mind that drives behavior and guides your choices. You can always choose to add different colors in order to change the entrepreneurial planet you occupy or further emphasize and reinforce your position. There are no wrong or right colors. Choose what your wisdom drives you to and what vibrates your soul. With every decision and experience, you, alone, color your talent and your masterpiece of self: thought by thought, intention by intention, and choice by choice. Always remember, you can add more colors!

"Color is the keyboard,
the eyes are the harmonies,
the soul is the piano with many strings.
The artist is the hand that plays,
touching one key or another,
to cause vibrations in the soul."

**—Wassily Kandinsky, Russian painter,
educator, lawyer, and father of abstract art**

---<>---

There are no correct or incorrect entrepreneurial states to occupy.

Those individuals less aware of their talents are the *sleeping giants*. Through stimulation, as a sleeping giant, you can *awaken and emerge*. You can also transition directly to a *practicing* entrepreneur through your guided aspiration and clear choices. At any given state, confusion can lead you to act foolishly or even become *misguided*, an often-destructive form of entrepreneurship.

You are in denial or unaware of your talents if you look at the Henry Fords of the world and

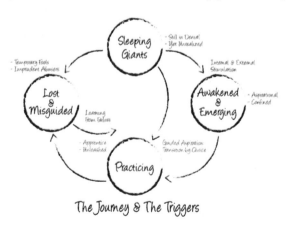

The Journey & The Triggers

see nothing in common. Your conclusion: if they are entrepreneurs, I certainly am not! They are risk-takers and players who swing for the fences and that is not me. You are rejecting your inherent entrepreneurial abilities, choosing to limit your capabilities, and therefore compromising your future. You hold all the potential offered by your talents, but are unaware of your daily exchange of resources for outcomes and the risks you are taking.

As a sleeping giant (in denial and unaware) you can change your entrepreneurial state through stimulation - an internal or external triggering event, sometimes caused by economic force of destitution or greed, that helps you see and appreciate your own talent. This entrepreneurial talent exists in all of us but it is your choice to stimulate it and apply it. When someone is born into a family of entrepreneurs and goes on to have a successful career, it is not genes that make them succeed, but the early encouragement that the family provides. To begin your journey from this state, start with stimulation.

If you define yourself as a sleeping giant and choose to change your state, the best route is to experiment with small exercises in order to stimulate your talents. To begin your state transition, consciously observe your daily affairs; see how you are constantly exchanging one thing, a resource, a service, or even an emotion for something you believe is of higher value. Realize that you are taking a risk in that exchange. Then acknowledge that, with increased knowledge, you can realize a more lucrative exchange. Aim to gain more knowledge in your daily exchanges and understand the risks better. This is how you begin to color your talent.

If you already consider yourself awakened and emerging, your entrepreneurial spirit is more aspirational but for some reason contained by your environment or corporate position. You are an aspirational entrepreneur when you realize your inherent potential. However, when it comes to commercial applications of your abilities, you operate in mostly after hours or weekend mode. You have discovered your abilities, but aim to limit your exposure to risk by restraining your commitments, suppressing your desires, and narrowing your efforts. If you find yourself to be aspirational, your biggest obstacle in the journey ahead is fear: of the unknown, of the hardship ahead, and of losing the comfort and the certainty of now. The biggest trap you face is false motivation and the so-called "proven paths" offered by thousands of "how-to" books which chip away at your originality. When it comes to becoming a practicing entrepreneur, skills and knowledge of the process are **absolutely critical** – they are the tires beneath your vehicle, without them you cannot roll. However, what fuels your vehicle and keeps you on the path is your distinctive approach to entrepreneurship (your very personal entrepreneurial philosophy or PEP) and your determination to apply its tenets. If aspirational, let your originality drive your transition. Never delegate coloring your entrepreneurial talent. You are the artist. Don't compromise your originality. You can learn the techniques of painting from others, but never let them steal your canvas.

"If you see a tree as blue, then make it blue."
—Paul Gauguin, 19th century French artist, unappreciated until after his death

Amir was a college student in Malaysia in the early 2000s. When his iPhone screen broke, he figured out a way to repair it himself. He also saw a way to make money. He discovered a market need and an opportunity to create and sell a screen repair kit on eBay. Faced with operational challenges, Amir quit the serendipitous business and focused on studying. At that point, he was an aspirational entrepreneur looking to make a few bucks while he worked through his plan to come to America, get a PhD, and a good job. Although he continued to pursue his original plan for a while, he later overcame his fear of failure and through guided aspiration fully unleashed his talents by founding a 3D printing technology company. He admits that the road he travelled has been filled with challenges, but his determination to seize opportunities has made him a practicing entrepreneur. (Additional information can be found in the *Harvard Business Review* case study, "SprintRay: Kick-starting Growth," by Sid Mohasseb and Divya Sathyanarayanan.)

Managers are entrepreneurs without the fancy label!

While working for corporate America, your aspirations may be contained by rules or boundaries which define your authority. Every day, you make decisions on using resources more effectively. With every decision, you place yourself and the company you work for at some level of risk. However, your decisions are constrained by the authority you are given. The more you expose your creativity, the more vulnerable you are within your organization. An intrapreneur operates within the confined limits of their organization, but often pushes the boundaries. When constrained, you may not get the opportunity to fully display your own entrepreneurial talents. Nevertheless, you can be a major force in running the engine of the economy. Every day, managers and employees around the world are innovating new processes and products in order to take advantage of opportunities and use their resources more effectively to achieve improved outcomes.

If you are forced or are choosing to break out and walk away from the comfort of employment, notice that many of the rules of the game are different. To win, reexamine your playbook. Look for biases you have developed over the years working within the big machine: planning is important, but execution is more important, all risks are very personal, your business card is no longer a door opener, your team matters much more than ever before, and people are not as easily replaceable. You should consider everything always in flux and be ready to pivot.

I was running an angel group in the mid-2000s. An angel group is comprised of investors who regularly convene to evaluate and invest in startup businesses. "Bob" approached the group for funding. He was a gem of a guy with significant industry experience; everyone loved him. He was laid off from his executive position at a large technology company and had decided to venture into entrepreneurship. He had an idea for a performance enhancing business-to-business software solution based on a market gap he had identified. When we met, he was a couple of years into his venture and had exhausted his savings. He had the shell of a software platform built by offshore developers, an impressive branding plan and material, but no customers. He had a couple of employees who were supporting his research and project managing the development process. Bob was playing the entrepreneurship game based on "corporate" rules – have a big vision, go through a long R&D process, build a solution, and use expensive resources to ensure proper branding and unveiling. Bob had a good business idea and was a loveable guy, but he had not received any money from investors because he failed to focus on incremental venture development and cash flow. Additionally, Bob seemed to be under extreme pressure from his family. He appeared to be looking for money to relieve his immediate pain and continue his venture using his old playbook. He was looking for others to take the cash flow burden off his shoulders as opposed to looking for a partner for growth. His approach to entrepreneurship was contained and that presented an investment risk. Everyone loved Bob, but no one invested in him!

Alternatively, Jeff Bezos had a lucrative career on Wall Street before transitioning to e-commerce and launching Amazon at age thirty-one. Jonah Peretti was a middle-school teacher before launching BuzzFeed and The Huffington Post in his thirties. Jeff and

Jonah revised the rules of the game as they transitioned from being contained to becoming fully practicing entrepreneurs.

Life, entrepreneurship, and learning are inseparable. To practice is to learn, and to learn is to practice.

As a practicing entrepreneur you unleash your talents by doing, but remain an apprentice by learning. You realize that you are always writing the next chapter of your life and are the sculptor of your next best version. You remain an apprentice of the craft and constantly position yourself to discover and apply your talents.

The psychological characteristics of practicing entrepreneurs are leadership and independence, as well as tolerance for ambiguity, change, and uncertainty. Practicing entrepreneurs are deemed to have a lower need for conformity and a higher propensity for risk-taking. This is the group often credited for major process or product innovations, new venture building, and job creation. When it comes to practicing entrepreneurs, the illusion of being "the one" is the single biggest reason for failure. You think, "I read a few books, made a few deals, and made some money; therefore, I am a full-fledged entrepreneur. I take risks, see opportunities, and my employees love me, therefore, I am an entrepreneur." But not one or a thousand successes makes a genuine practicing entrepreneur complete. A practicing entrepreneur continues to experiment with colors in order to learn more and get more from their talent.

All practicing entrepreneurs remain apprentices!

At any state, entrepreneurs can become misguided and begin to regress — a journey towards destruction. The imprudent, intentionally or not, are confused about how to use their inherent entrepreneurial talent. Some misguided entrepreneurs abuse their talents, others are temporary fools. Abusers include the old "snake oil salesmen" who, under the umbrella of entrepreneurship, declare all fraudulent activities fair game. Some are the con artists, wolves in sheep's clothing, and others are reckless and impulsive. Abusers often try to "fake it until they make it" and are constantly looking for a fast buck. Elizabeth Holmes, the founder of Theranos, a now-defunct company known for its false claim of having revolutionized blood testing, initially hyped the start-up unicorn company as a breakthrough technology firm. She raised over $700 million from venture investors. She was hoping that, with time, she could fulfill the claims made about the company's capabilities while faking it by using the same old machines. Time ran out! She miscalculated the risks and then doubled and tripled down on the failure by how she managed the crisis. Theranos dissolved in September, 2018, and Holmes was indicted by a federal grand jury for having engaged in efforts to defraud investors, doctors, and patients.

Abusers are aiming to take advantage of situations. Temporary fools, however, are most destructive to themselves and often successful only by luck. Fools are more like gamblers. They don't navigate through risks; they just take them. They follow their passion blindly without considering outcomes. I admit I have been a fool at least once or twice during my journey. In fact, most practicing entrepreneurs have crossed the line. The authentic ones are also willing to admit it.

If you are an abuser, you have made your choice. One can hope that failure and learning could guide you back to a more productive state. If a fool, you are wasting your inherent talent for greatness — learn fast and make your foolishness as short-lived as you can. You have a choice.

---<>---

The fact is:
all entrepreneurs can and
often do change their state.
You will, too.

Which state of entrepreneurship you occupy at any given time is entirely your choice. You control the color palette and only you can choose the colors you add to your pure entrepreneurial talent. As the world changes or as you influence its change, you occupy the state of entrepreneurship most meaningful to you and your growth. You must discover your entrepreneurial state of mind, but realize that when it comes to life and entrepreneurship, there are no permanent states. Nothing in the world is static, including you. Wherever you are positioned today, you have or may run the spectrum in the future, not once, but over and over. Be always aware of the mental stumbling blocks that limit the rainbow of your colors and choices.

> *"It is the eye of ignorance*
> *that assigns a fixed and unchangeable color to every object;*
> *beware of this stumbling block."*
> **—Paul Gauguin, 19th century French artist,**
> **recognized for his experimental use of color**

In some circumstances you may be unaware of your talents or are in denial. On other occasions you may be aspirational but contained and fearful of the choices and consequences you face. In some situations, you may have to fight hard to overcome your entanglement with greed or ego in order to avoid becoming misguided. When facing certain projects or circumstances, you may act foolish. Every practicing entrepreneur has, at one time or another, been a temporary fool! Travelling through the galaxy and the various states of entrepreneurship is natural and often essential to learning and growth.

---<>---

Next, position yourself to learn, but do not be a copy.

Your state of entrepreneurship may very well resemble someone else. However, be very careful. **YOU ARE NOT THEM!**

CHAPTER SEVEN:

YOU ARE NOT THEM!

"Knowing others is intelligence;
knowing yourself is true wisdom.
Mastering others is strength;
mastering yourself is true power."
—Lao Tzu, Chinese philosopher

Entrepreneurs get bombarded with generic advice all the time: embrace failure, follow your passion, know when and how to say no, balance work and life, build an effective team, be curious and, my personal favorite, think big. Generic one-liners may sound inspiring, but are often not practical. Following your passion does not necessarily guarantee your success and being constantly curious without purpose can lead you down the wrong path. Failure is not inherently a good thing when you don't have millions in Venture Capital (VC) money in the bank, and thinking too big, too early, can lead to your demise. Advice is both valuable and actionable only when it resonates with your Personalized Entrepreneurial Philosophy (PEP).

Sophocles, the Greek author, pronounced over 3,000 years ago, "No enemy is worse than bad advice." Other entrepreneurs may be sympathetic or claim to understand your situation; however, none of us is truly qualified to prescribe what you should do in any given circumstance. Simply put: we are not you! Your entire package of experiences, your originality, and your origins are unique. We can offer advice on what we would do in a similar situation based on our perspective on who you are – which may be biased, our take on your description of the situation – often one-sided and unreliable hearsay, and knowing that whatever the outcome, we will not suffer the consequences. You will.

The goalposts for entrepreneurs move all the time. In the 19th century, entrepreneurs were powerful figures who built industries: bigger than life characters, like Andrew Carnegie in the steel industry, Cornelius Vanderbilt building railroads, J. P. Morgan shaping the financial industry, and John D. Rockefeller, the oil tycoon. Later, the focus of entrepreneurship shifted from conquest to management – methods of improvement, functions, and business education. The decline of the economy in the 1970s and 80s fueled a renewed need for catalysts for growth and innovation. Practicing entrepreneurs powered the engine of the economy and nurtured the small business. Bill Gates at Microsoft, Steve Jobs at Apple, and Larry Ellison at Oracle shined during this era, as they built and popularized computers and software. Sam Walton reshaped the discount retail industry via Walmart and Ted Turner revolutionized entertainment by making CNN the center of a paid television network. The 21st century carries the legacy of Jeff Bezos of Amazon and Jack Ma of Alibaba in China – entrepreneurs who are using technology to cross industries and break barriers.

Every one of these entrepreneurs is entirely different. They lived in different eras, faced different limitations, conquered unique opportunities, and had a different risk profile. Each of them, as well as the millions who operated smaller enterprises – the corner stores, the cab companies, the restaurateurs and manufacturers – have their unique challenges and opportunities. Looking ahead, post COVID-19, there will be new challenges created by a "contact free" economy, an economy that may promise reduced physical contacts but will, without a doubt, deliver tremendously increased digital connections. New business and personal complications lie ahead that will have to be tackled by entrepreneurs across every industry; trials and tribulations that have never been seen before and opportunities that have never been defined or imagined. Ahead lies nationalism, environmental challenges, larger gaps between the rich and poor, possible dominance by machines and artificial intelligence. All challenges that entrepreneurs will have to navigate through; challenges that are pregnant with opportunities never before seen.

What lies ahead is always entirely different than what has been.

Life before jet engine planes, electricity, 9/11 and the iPhone was vastly different from life after these inventions. Life after the COVID-19 pandemic will also be different. It will be filled with new promises and new entrepreneurs with fresh perspectives. The next generation that can examine and learn from those that preceded it, but will never be exactly like them or face the exact same challenges.

----<>----

As you remain open to receiving advice and examining other entrepreneurs, **first acknowledge** that you are not them. **Next, gain the knowledge** that is essential to color your entrepreneurial talent and fuel your choices.

"Knowledge is in the end based on acknowledgement."
—Ludwig Wittgenstein, Austrian-British philosopher

John D. Rockefeller held the belief, "The growth of large business is merely a survival of the fittest." His philosophy favored industry monopolization, a perspective that seems to be shared by Peter Theil, the founder of PayPal and a major investor of Facebook. In contrast, Andrew Carnegie, a primary rival to Rockefeller, believed that business success is ingrained in cooperation and learning how to combine diversified resources. His philosophy was rooted in his belief that guided collaboration allows common people to attain uncommon results.

Coco Chanel, like Steve Jobs, had a reputation for perfectionism. Like Andrew Carnegie, she believed in building connections. Her belief in learning, always through books, was closer to the sentiments of Bill Gates and Warren Buffet. Buffet also believes in having discipline. The legendary investor's philosophy emphasizes knowledge, integrity, intelligent risk mitigation, and value creation. He claims that "to win," you need emotional stability coupled with independent thinking and action. Follow facts and reasoning. In contrast, Steve Jobs believed, "There is no reason not to follow your heart." He valued intuition and experiential wisdom more than intelligence, research, or learned knowledge. He was known to value creativity and risk. He believed, "It's not the customer's job to know what they want." Jobs' fierce rival, Bill Gates, a self-proclaimed impatient optimist, believes, "Your most unhappy customers are your greatest source of learning." He knew that getting people to tell you what you're doing wrong is the best way to learn what needs improvement.

Bezos always ends his annual letters to Amazon shareholders with the short, but powerful statement: "It is Day One." He hints that we should stay frugal and continue to build and to learn because opportunities are still ahead. Bezos suggests, "Stay terrified of your customers." He emphasizes that a company's risk appetite should scale as it grows; he proclaims that "wandering is the counterbalance to efficiency." Bezos, like Richard Branson of Virgin Airlines, believes that employees' roles should never be overlooked. He claims a company must create "a culture of builders, people who are curious explorers." This enables employees to shape its future and adopt a culture of ownership because "when they feel ownership, they think and act in the long term."

Successful entrepreneurs have one thing in common: they are "not alike." Unsuccessful entrepreneurs also have one thing in common: they aim to be "like" others.

Always remember, regardless of whom you mentally resonate with, admire, or appreciate, you are not them!

Every one of these iconic and accomplished practicing entrepreneurs has a philosophy that drives their cohesive and coordinated strategies, decisions, choices, actions, and reactions. Study them and learn from them, not because you want to be like them, but to discover what wisdom uniquely applies to you. They are great entrepreneurs because they have their own unique philosophy fine-tuned to who they are.

To own your future, start by carving your personal philosophy. A philosophy that works for you and you alone. Realize that other entrepreneurs enjoy their own viewpoints. Perspectives that are anchored in their core beliefs influenced by their origins, experiences, and capabilities. Philosophies that fit the environment and times they live in. Philosophies that guide their choices, but not necessarily yours.

Learn, but never be a copy!

---<>---

Before you start adding more colors to your entrepreneurial talent or decide who you resonate with, be prepared to shape your own Personal Entrepreneurial Philosophy.

Go beyond the motivational taglines of blindly pursuing your passion. Next, **PURSUE YOUR LOVE** of your wisdom!

CHAPTER EIGHT:

PURSUE YOUR LOVE

Learn the love of wisdom
from every tree.

A tree is a tree.
It is always authentic
and genuine, down to its roots
free but defined;
always evolving, searching
for growth yet
grounded forever,
reaching for the sun.

Strong in storms,
bending with the winds,
patient with winter
and impatient in spring;
Transforming to renew
unbound by the past.

Be like a tree
with sturdy roots,
traveling the distance
in search of the flow.
Help your leaves grow,
learn to let them go.
Cultivate your fruits,
But stand ready to share
with patience and care.

Love your wisdom just like a tree.
It is your wisdom
that will make you
who you will be!
A wise, unique tree.

The term philosophy literally means "love of wisdom." It is the study of fundamental questions of life, knowledge, values, and reason. A Personal Entrepreneurial Philosophy (PEP) deals with exploration, acceptance, and the practice of your love of wisdom as applied to your entrepreneurial talent. A thinking and doing platform that is erected based on who you are.

To pursue your PEP is to embody your beliefs. It is to live them and evolve with them. It is a perpetual hunt for next choices and consequences. It is a pursuit that never ends. Your PEP is the mental manifesto that universally guides your decisions and actions. It includes what may be categorically imperative (accepted universal moral truths, according to the German philosopher Immanuel Kant), but it also includes the ideas and approaches that are universally and uniquely applied by you. A kind of universality that is valid until disputed and improved by you alone, as a part of your evolution. Your PEP is your unique collection of "First Principles," or, as Aristotle defines them, basic propositions or assumptions that cannot be further deduced. The evolving principles that collectively define how you approach situations, view choices, make decisions, and deal with consequences. Principles that are further enhanced with learning. The evolving viewpoint that shapes each next best version of you.

---<>---

Your PEP is an ever-evolving wisdom that influences your thinking and doing.

Your PEP is shaped by your priorities, views on creativity, leadership, inclusion and risk tolerance. It is influenced by your previous success patterns, upbringing, societal impacts, and character strengths and flaws.

While your core beliefs, morality and value system will, without a doubt, influence your PEP, they are NOT equal to it. You may believe that all humans are equal, but employees are judged differently based on their contribution and value to the organization. You may believe in a Zen-like acceptance and conflict avoidance doctrine, but your PEP may drive you towards not accepting failure as a permanent status and embracing conflict when your organization's livelihood depends on it. Your core beliefs cannot and should not be avoided, but they cannot replace your PEP. Your PEP drives you to learn and refine. It helps influence the probability of success in your favor. **Your core beliefs may drive who you are, but your PEP is the framework that guides you to become who you can "BE."**

Your wisdom reveals itself when the "known" clashes with the "unknown" and when change is at work and choices appear.

"Wisdom is the crown of the kings,
the honor of the heroes
The wise, the artist declares:
That who does not pursue her wisdom,
will regret her actions."
—Ferdowsi, Persian poet and philosopher

---<>---

It is time to hug, clinch, cuddle, and hold your talent. It is time to claim it and to color it. Time to bless the marriage of your choices with change. The time to explore the galaxy of entrepreneurship and pursue your love of your wisdom.

*"The hours of folly are measured by the clock;
but of wisdom, no clock can measure."*
—William Blake, English poet

It is time: **IGNITE AND "BE."** Choose to "BE" or not to "BE"!

Next, embrace your origin as you discover your originality. Being an entrepreneur is independent of your origin, however being an original is most definitely influenced by it.

Next, explore the journey from **ORIGIN TO ORIGINALITY.**

<<END OF PART TWO>>

PART THREE: IGNITE & BE

TO BE OR NOT TO BE!

That is NOT a Question …
It is a Choice.

CHAPTER NINE:

FROM ORIGIN TO ORIGINALITY

"For years my heart inquired of me:
Where Jamshid's sacred cup might be?
What was in its own possession
It asked from stranger, where could it be?"
—Hafez, Persian poet and philosopher

We all have different origins- our starting points are different and our capabilities vary. We each experience a different journey. A voyage that begins from a point that we presumably had no role in choosing, on a path that is constructed by our own choices. An excursion that begins with dissimilarity of backgrounds and personality traits, and continues with dissimilarity of choices and consequences.

Along the way, whether we choose to follow or lead, we are building an original life – our version of being, competing, growing, learning, and leading. Our unique manifestation of individual entrepreneurial talents.

When it comes to entrepreneurship and leadership, all is relative. Original and authentic entrepreneurs are able to turn what is relative into what is relevant to the situations they are in. That is how you can make your inherent talent shine. Great entrepreneurs and leaders seek to learn not only to understand what is, but to architect what can become. Wherever your origins, at the edges of who you are today is the unique and original "YOU" waiting to be discovered.

In life and in entrepreneurship aim to create and not just find yourself.

---<>---

There is no question that uncontrollable factors impact the twin talents of entrepreneurship and leadership. Family wealth provides the luxury of access to qualified "paid" experts, specialists who can protect against bad decisions. Wealth often allows the offspring of aristocrats to inherit and not earn leadership; some get to lead because they are the son or daughter of an important person or because they can buy themselves a leadership position. Combined with social status, the wealthy have access to better education, tools, and training.

Preestablished success circles breed more success, more wealth, influence, and access. Without question, that is an advantage. However, your entrepreneurship and leadership talents are no more or less than others because of those advantages. Each person is born with a certain level of intellect. Higher intelligence is most definitely another advantage. Moreover, the society and the environment you live in somewhat paints the scope of your growth and the nature of the opportunities available to you. Notwithstanding, neither intellect nor society diminishes the entrepreneurship and leadership talents you hold within.

There are thousands of examples of people who became leaders because of a combination of uncontrollable factors - examples of incompetence and failure. Uncontrollable factors may increase the odds of being placed in a leadership position, but they do not guarantee effective success.

You may not always be able to build the future you want, but you can build yourself to conquer the future ahead.

Margaret Roberts, the daughter of a Methodist preacher and a grocery shop owner, was born in 1925, a few years after World War I ended and a little more than a decade before World War II began. Margaret graduated with a degree in chemistry from the University of Oxford in 1947. She applied for a job as a chemist, but was rejected after the personnel department assessed her as "headstrong, obstinate and dangerously self-opinionated." At age twenty-four, she faced multiple defeats as a Conservative Party candidate. She married at the age of twenty-five and became known as Margaret Thatcher. She became a member of Parliament in 1959 at the age of thirty-three.

In 1970, Thatcher was appointed as Secretary of State for Education and Science. That same year, some started suggesting she could become prime minister, to which she replied: "There will not be a woman prime minister in my lifetime – the male population is too prejudiced." Five years later, Thatcher became Leader of the Opposition as the Conservative Party leader. Slowly she became the face of the ideological movement, opposing the British welfare state. Keynesian economics, she believed, was weakening Britain. The ideology was rooted in less government, lower taxes, and more freedom for business and consumers. In early 1979, the Conservatives won a majority in the House of Commons and Thatcher - the "Iron Lady," as the Soviets later called her, became the first female British prime minister.

During her first year in office the Soviets invaded Afghanistan and an Islamic revolution changed the power dynamics in the Middle East. By the third year, she had ordered war against Argentina as the aggressor in the Falkland Islands and was actively negotiating with the Chinese over the sovereignty of Hong Kong. She survived torturous economic recessions and massive riots, but stayed steadfast to her conservative economic beliefs. She was strongly for privatization and adamantly against socialism and trade unions. She believed, "There is no such thing as public money; there is only taxpayers' money." When people asked for her to turn back her policies, she publicly proclaimed, "You turn if you want to. The lady's not for turning." By the end of 1980, her approval rating had fallen below twenty-four percent. But, by 1987, she was reelected for the third time.

Thatcher was an original with strong beliefs. She came from humble beginnings, grew up in a rural town, yet eventually became Britain's first woman prime minister. She prospered, despite the disadvantages of her origins – being a woman in a predominately male-oriented society and not being from an aristocratic family. Like every original leader, she faced hardship and challenges along the way. She experienced defeat and opposition, even to the point of an Irish Republican Army (IRA) assassination attempt. She was a poor public speaker and always rough around the edges, but she was able to preserve her uniqueness and tap into new personality traits that were needed to effectively express her leadership talent.

During her premiership, at an average of forty percent, Thatcher had the second lowest approval rating of any post-war prime minister. She was made a Baroness and took a seat in the House of Lords in 1992. Yet Thatcherism, "the belief that economic freedom and individual liberty are interdependent and that personal responsibility and hard work are the only ways to national prosperity, and that the free-market democracies must stand firm against aggression — had won many disciples" (*New York Times*, April 9, 2013). She was loved by some and disliked by others. Some even claim that she awakened Britain to a new dawn. Regardless of your views, her journey from her origins and her path to discovering her originality offers valuable lessons. All people are born and eventually die, but not all truly live. Margaret Roberts Thatcher died in 2013. She was an original who lived to leave a legacy.

Don't let uncompromising circumstances crush your inherent talents and make you a victim. Conversely, don't be fooled: a leadership position you inherit is neither necessarily what you deserve nor the limit of your capabilities. Choose to be the original you and create new circumstances in which to thrive. You possess all that you need within you. Choose to express your entrepreneurial talent. God may define your origins, but you are responsible for discovering your originality.

"It's choice - not chance - that determines your destiny."
—Jean Evelyn Nidetch, American business entrepreneur, founder of the Weight Watchers organization

---<>---

Personality traits influence how leadership is expressed. No one can dispute that each one of us has a different combination of traits, traits that makes us engage with others and approach situations differently.

When it comes to entrepreneurship and personality traits, it can easily be proved that correlation is not causation. Not all who have certain personality traits are great leaders and entrepreneurs and not everyone who lacks them is unable to lead.

Carl Jung, a Swiss psychiatrist, psychoanalyst, and the father of analytical psychology, argued that all personality traits are present in an individual and the dominant trait might vary by situation. It means that each of us has the ability to be an extrovert and an introvert, be agreeable or disagreeable, be fickle or reliable, be talkative or reserved, etc. Accordingly, we are all able to express our entrepreneurship through our situationally chosen personality traits. Traits that are flexible channels of expression and communication. Traits that guide how you express yourself in certain situations.

All personality traits sit on a continuum and none produce infinite entrepreneurship or leadership abilities. To be effective, you have to learn to apply the right trait to the right conditions. Since both entrepreneurship and leadership are situational, the channels of your expressions (your traits) must also be situational. You must express yourself in a manner that fits the situation and leads to desired outcomes. Effective leadership is not about the absolute presence or absence of particular personality traits. It is about your individual ability to let your talents reveal themselves at the right time in the right situation.

You are a manifestation of your adopted and inherited traits.

How you express and materialize yourself is who you are. Learn to apply the right traits to the right situations and leadership opportunities. Practice your unique brand of entrepreneurship. Choose to become the authentic YOU. Choose to want more from yourself and your ecosystem; choose to inspire and be inspired.

To stimulate your wanderlust, you must face and ignite change. To create your originality and travel the jagged path of life and business, you must choose to apply your entrepreneurial talent. You must get to the edge of what you know and cross over it into a new territory of knowledge. To construct your originality and evolve, you must learn to constantly exchange what you have with something better while considering the risks.

---<>---

"When you come to the edge of all that you know,
you must believe one of two things:
either there will be ground to stand on,
or you will be given wings to fly."
—O.R. Melling, author

Next, learn to **BE A PILOT**.

To discover your authentic self, you must confidently choose to exchange who you have been with who you can become; you must risk!

Through an exchange of a state, an idea, a situation, or a resource for something better, knowing that nothing is for certain, is how you create your next best version, one decision at a time. All in life and entrepreneurship is subject to chance; all decisions are entangled with risk!

Risk is always looming and you must constantly navigate it like **a pilot**.

CHAPTER TEN:

BE A PILOT

Risk is at the center of every decision and your decisions shape who you are. You choose movement, action, and progress when you elect to take a risk. You also take a risk when you choose sameness and inaction. You take a risk when you leave your home without an umbrella, when you drive to work, when you exercise at the gym, or when you have a drink. You take a risk if you are a startup entrepreneur, an executive at a conglomerate, a student, a teacher, or a fireman. You take a risk whether you are the pilot or a passenger on a flight.

Rule number one of life and entrepreneurship: **choose** to take risks!

Despite popular belief, skilled entrepreneurs are not imprudent risk takers; they choose to be pilots and navigators.

Without risk, there is no life. To avoid risk is to avoid life. Innovation, creativity, and evolution are but a dream, without risk.

John Paul Jones, the U.S. naval commander during the American Revolutionary War, stated, "It seems to be a law of nature, inflexible and inexorable, that those who will not risk cannot win." You can choose to be a pilot (an active participant) or a passenger (a passive one). The risk of a crash is present either way! Aircraft pilots would be grounded forever if they always chose safety and certainty.

Passengers trust the pilots to take the wheel and navigate the risks. But you still risk, even as a passenger. Employees choose to have their leadership mitigate the risks associated with their professional life. They trust their higher-ups to steer the organization and provide them with job security, career growth, meaningful work, and, of course, a paycheck.

Rule number two of life and entrepreneurship: navigate risk!

When it comes to their personal lives, passengers are actually pilots, risk takers, and entrepreneurs. From the time you are born, you are programmed to explore uncertainty and embrace risk; you are designed to evaluate options, assess risks, and choose. You decide how you evolve. You are constantly steering your life through a minefield of choices and consequences. You are a pilot; you choose to embrace risk and navigate towards prosperity. Because, if you choose not to risk, you choose not to exist!

No risk equals no journey, stagnation, and demise. Not to risk is to risk it all!

---<>---

CONFIDENT NAVIGATORS

When you confidently navigate risk like a pilot, you choose to blossom as an entrepreneur.

"And the day came when the risk to remain tight in a bud was more painful than the risk it took to blossom."
— Anais Nin, French-born poet and author

Pilots are aware of the hazards of every trip and willingly embrace them. A bird can fly into the engine and prompt disaster. A single, inexpensive diode, capacitor, or memory chip can drive system failure. And yet every day pilots choose to fly because they are confident risk navigators who prefer movement to stillness.

The U.S. Department of Transportation Federal Aviation Administration's (FAA) handbook for risk management states that "identifying threats and exposures and the associated risk in time is key to addressing vulnerabilities." If a pilot fails to search for risk, it is likely that he or she will neither see it nor appreciate it for what it represents. Unfortunately, in aviation, pilots have a much smaller margin for error and do not have the opportunity to learn if the mistakes happen to be fatal. Entrepreneurs may enjoy a bit less life and death pressure on their flights. However, life and business pressures amplify as the speed of change and innovation constantly increases.

Travis Kalanick, the founder of Uber, made his company vulnerable and was pressured to resign as the CEO in 2017 because of the company's supposedly unethical culture. Travis was a *misguided* entrepreneur: he facilitated spying on passengers, dubious driverless-car experiments, and price gouging through nighttime price surge algorithms — all non-mitigated risks in hopes of raising revenue and valuation. He clearly miscalculated the threat and the exposure associated with his risky behavior. Uber did go public in 2019 and raised over $8 billion. But, as of the first part of 2020, the company shows a loss of close to $8.5 billion in a year. Travis did make a lot of money and is now starting a new company. But none of that alleviates his role in placing the company at unwarranted risk. The competitive business world has become an unforgiving arena and errors in judgement routinely come back to haunt entrepreneurs and their companies. Consider John Stumpf, the chairman and CEO of Wells Fargo, who had to resign when the company was caught boosting performance by opening bogus accounts. The bank may have enjoyed some good times in the market, but risk caught up with the CEO and the entire executive team. As a pilot, an entrepreneur, you not only have to identify the threats that surround you, but also have to avoid becoming the source of risk. In entrepreneurship, there are only momentary perfect conditions to fly. A storm is always on the horizon. Be prepared for one, but don't rush to face it without cause.

> *"You learn to know a pilot in a storm."*
> **—Seneca, Roman philosopher**

Pilots often have support from people on the ground, the crew on board, and the air traffic controllers along the way. However, according to the FAA, pilots accept their own individual level of risk even though they have received similar training. Risk, which must be managed individually, becomes a problem when the situation's complexity exceeds the pilot's capability (background + education + predispositions + attitude + training). The key to managing risk is the pilot's understanding of the threshold and perception of the risk. In other words, the nature and degree of risk exposure changes from person to person; the same applies to entrepreneurs. Entrepreneurs have a list of common things to worry about (employees, cash flow, product launches, customer loyalty, etc.), but the extent and impact of the risk stemming from each varies from entrepreneur to entrepreneur, company to company, and situation to situation. The conditions that exist or appear during a flight are neither wrong nor right. What makes all the difference in the world, however, is the way a pilot navigates and mitigates the risks. The same goes for entrepreneurs who navigate the competitive world.

There are countless dangers in life and in business;
the biggest is the illusion of safety and blindness to the reality of risk.

---<>---

YOU REAP WHAT YOU SOW!

Your decisions define you and risk defines your decisions. With every choice, you pave your own unique path to the future. With every judgement, you place yourself in a situation, take a position, and evolve as you act and face the consequences of your choices; your decisions, therefore, define you. They shape your ever-evolving sculpture of self.

Behind every decision you make there are choices, analyses and rationalizations, alternatives and expected outcomes. You assess the risks associated with alternatives and the likely consequences and commit to a decision by accepting a level of risk. It is, therefore, risk that defines your decisions.

You define your risks and your choices and cause your consequences; you reap what you sow!

The FAA outlines risk around the four categories of i) **Pilot**: physical and emotional health, fatigue, medication, and stress; ii) **Aircraft**: conditions of the plane, payload, instrumentation, fuel, passengers, etc.); iii) **Environment**: weather conditions, terrain at airports, and day and night differences; iv) **External Pressures**: personal life, co-workers, bosses, etc. Entrepreneurial risks can also be defined by similar categories.

Pilot: Entrepreneur

Entrepreneurs who burn the candle at both ends (work extremely or excessively hard) often become a source of risk. This is not about the always essential "hard work." Risk is created when decision-making abilities are compromised. In a world of fierce competition, it is often critical to push ourselves and our teams to the limit. However, as we do this, we are increasing our risks. Good pilots avoid flying when their judgement is impaired. In 2018, Elon Musk, the high-flying founder of SpaceX and X.com (now PayPal), as well as an early investor in Tesla, pushed himself to the point of being impaired. In an interview with *The New York Times*, he said, "This past year has been the most difficult and painful year of my career. It was excruciating." No one can question his genius, but his decision to push himself to exhaustion led to the creation of unnecessary risks – unfounded claims of taking the company private and causing mistrust in the market by appearing drunk while smoking a marijuana joint. These were all pointless, fabricated risks. *Entrepreneurial risks are often catalyzed by the entrepreneurs themselves.*

In the early 1990s, my partner, Dan Straub, and I were commissioned by the Administrative Offices of the Courts of California and Chief Justice George. The mission was to plan for a massive consolidation of the Superior and Municipal Courts of California, going from over two hundred independent entities to fifty-eight. We designed a number of tools and methods to help re-engineer processes and streamline the staffing and budgeting activities; these tools turned into a software called RAM (Resource Allocation Model). I proposed the software solution idea to one of the court CEOs. I suggested that the court hire software developers to code it. Despite my insistence that we were not a software development company, the client maintained that we should build it for them! Eventually, I agreed. I called my partner to let him know of our planned journey into the software development world. He immediately claimed, "You always take off with the plane before building the landing gear."

This comment has stayed with me for close to thirty years. Obviously, the approach creates risk. However, I have learned that market timing, funding limitations, and customer expectations sometimes demand it. To take off without the landing gear suggests that the entrepreneur has assessed the probability of success - designing, building, and installing the proper landing apparatus while in flight. It also signals a degree of confidence in their team's and partners' (ecosystem's) abilities. The software solution was eventually deployed to ninety-six courts, spawning a separate company which was sold a few years later.

In a conversation with an aspiring and extremely competent entrepreneur who was looking for funding, I was reminded that entrepreneurs often fail to take off without landing gear even when it is critical to do so. They lack the confidence to fly; simply, they are afraid. This individual had raised close to $2 million for her venture some months before, but was still waiting to start the full force execution by hiring people and initiating FDA (Food & Drug Administration) related tests. She was waiting until she got another $500k and secured an 18-month run rate. She was waiting for all the parts of the plane to be constructed and tested before gaining enough confidence to start the journey. This approach is wrong! Don't evade risk and foolishly expect certainty. Entrepreneurs don't duck for cover when faced with uncertainty; they navigate and mitigate the risks. She failed to raise the additional capital as investors awaited signs of execution and results. Eventually, she started to execute with force and realized that uncertainty and entrepreneurship go hand in hand. A year later, she was able to raise another $3 million with relative ease as investors observed her ability to produce results.

Good entrepreneurs know how to navigate risk. They realize when to take risks by assessing their capabilities realistically and learn how to mitigate them by using the expertise, knowledge, and visions of others, e.g., their investors, partners, employees, and customers. Choose from whom you take advice carefully and then genuinely listen. Take advice only from people you trust and who are competent about the topic, objective, and resonate with your PEP.

Always remember, not all advice is good or relevant. Every basketball player should listen to the coaches and not be distracted by the fans, regardless of how loud they yell. As an entrepreneur, choose your advisors carefully and listen genuinely. Also, remember that there are no perfect pilots and that all pilots have to be trained in steps.

"He who would learn to fly one day must first learn to stand and walk and run and climb and dance; one cannot fly into flying."
—Friedrich Nietzsche, German philosopher

The Aircraft: The Entity

The company you build is the vessel that holds the ability to turn your vision into a product, a service offering, or a business. Every company is glued together by processes and technology, people and culture, and strategy and mission. At every connection point, risk is concealed. Processes can break, technologies can malfunction, security can be breached, people can be dismayed, and customers disheartened. There is always a probability of risk emerging. To be able to mitigate the risks, you must first be aware and then act. As the entrepreneur, your aim is comprehensive understanding of sources and probabilities of risks. Although you may aim to understand ALL sources of risk, you have to realize that perfection is only a myth and never truly achievable. You have to be ready to ride the probabilities. Practicing entrepreneurs focus on critical execution steps and rely on technology, their team, advisors, and a supportive ecosystem to inform them of anomalies pointing to risk – like a pilot and his cockpit instrumentation.

The Environment: The Economy, the Market, and the Competition

The economy, market, and competition risks are never 100 percent known or contained! You cannot avoid them, but you can learn to navigate them. The competitive world is a multidimensional chess game with risk hiding in every move. Risk generated by each pawn, rook, knight, bishop, queen, and king: the economy, constantly changing customer expectations, technology advances, innovation from across the globe, trade wars, and more. These risks have been the domain of entrepreneurs forever. They are mostly known and explored by skillful MBAs. The soybean farmers affected by the Chinese trade war, iPhone losing market share to Samsung's Android, and Delta, American, and United Airlines looking victorious (prior to the COVID-19 pandemic of 2020, of course) after bloody price wars are representative of risks induced by the environment. The environment is uncertain and infested with risk. Be aware of it, master dynamic mitigation, and position yourself to win. Risk is dynamic. The Theory of Games is an illusion of predictability as it assumes that all parties in a competitive situation (markets) will behave logically. As one company or market moves, others react, and their reactions are based on their strategies and assumptions, not yours! Be on the lookout for illogical moves.

The External Pressure: The Stakeholders

Ignore the external pressures and you will be dangerously exposed!

Three newly minted entrepreneurs were seeking a $5 million dollar capital investment. Their stated objectives were to quit their jobs, focus on the project, and not worry about their familial obligations. They claimed to have solved a big problem for small retail business owners, particularly restaurants, and believed that their company was worth $20 million. They intended to build a platform retailers could use to promote their offers and daily specials and manage their reviews (eliminate bad ones). They were three successful individuals: an executive at Google, a management consultant with retail market experience, and an expert in agile technology development. They claimed to be fully committed and had invested a total of $15,000 in the company. First of all, in this day and age, $15k is not a sign that three high level executives are committed to a cause or sharing the risk. Second, risk cannot be shifted to investors to protect families and obligations; it can be mitigated, but not unloaded on someone else. Lastly, asking for a large investment at such high valuation with a first draft app and no active customers is simply unreasonable.

To be a pilot, you must be prepared to fly and anticipate external pressures. You will pressure the family bonds constantly as you inject uncertainty into their day-to-day lives and split your time and attention between them and others. To be a practicing entrepreneur is to be prepared to expose your family to financial risk. You should also realize that the objective of getting investors is not only to reduce your personal risk, but to increase the probability of your company's success. By taking money from investors, you have not eliminated your risk, but exposed yourself to a different set of challenges around execution and timing imposed by them.

In addition to friends and family-imposed difficulties, external pressures also extend themselves to other parts of your ecosystem. Your employees are your key stakeholders. They can get sick, get tired, or quit- risk, risk, and more risk. On top of that, social norms and expectations offer even more risks.

Regardless of source,
in aviation, just as in business,
a successful journey is not the result of
eliminating risk,
but a conscious decision to be
prepared for it
and the ability to navigate around it
...or at times through it.

---<>---

NOT ALL PILOTS OR FLIGHTS ARE EQUAL

Being a pilot requires risk management on every flight. However, the nature and level of risk varies based on the purpose of the journey. Standard air traffic categories of flights and pilots include general aviation, commercial aviation, and military. General aviation mostly involves small aircraft used for leisure and corporate charters. A majority of pilots (over eighty percent) in America fly general aviation aircraft and, of those, a considerable number are joyriders and weekend flyers. Commercial aviators are involved with larger commercially purposed air travel facilitated by airlines or cargo companies. Military pilots, who are often the most skilled risk navigators, operate a range of aircraft, including fighter jets, bombers, and helicopters.

Then we have the very elite group of pilots: the astronauts. Trailblazers like Valentina Tereshkova, the first woman to travel into space and safely return to Earth. Astronauts are highly trained and battlefield tested. They have thousands of hours of flying under their belt and show superior physical and mental ability. They are the few who are willing to risk everything to discover, to truly go where no man has gone before, as Star Trek fans would put it. They are fighter jet pilots who have a mission to serve mankind. In entrepreneurship, some consider Elon Musk, Jeff Bezos, and Jack Ma a similar elite group. They navigate through extreme risk to realize grandiose and less probable outcomes.

A casual weekend flyer deals with a less sophisticated aircraft and their failure may represent, except for the specific aviator themselves, a lesser disaster than a commercial aviator responsible for hundreds of lives every day on every trip across the globe. While casual pilots are often thrill seekers and joyriders, commercial pilots are serious and focused professionals. In entrepreneurship, the aspiring entrepreneurs who build things or sell things as a hobby enjoy the flight as weekend flyers; they are pilots, but have chosen to limit their exposure to risk. The large corporate executives whose entrepreneurial talents are confined face some level of risk at their jobs. They are pilots, but their flights are more routine, the dangers are less personal, and the corporate structure and financial muscle offer them shelter. They are more like commercial pilots.

Fighter pilots are the most exposed warriors, constantly trained and ready for a dogfight. They often push the "bingo fuel" and get close to the minimum fuel needed to fly back home safely. These pilots are schooled to maneuver skillfully (similar to pivoting as an entrepreneur to sidestep failure) to avoid hostile fire while flying at high speed. They soar for a purpose that is much greater than themselves – their countries and a way of life. Committed early stage entrepreneurs are more like fighter pilots. They not only have to manage the regular risks of flying (business), but also face a fast-moving and innovative competitive world without the safety offered by a big corporate blanket. Pledged entrepreneurs have a bigger purpose than joy or money (making a living) – they have a cause and a solid foundation of beliefs. They prefer to fight and die for something over merely surviving and living for nothing.

"You don't concentrate on risks.
You concentrate on results.
No risk is too great to
prevent the necessary job from getting done."
—Chuck Yeager, U.S. Air Force officer,
first man to break the speed of sound

Military pilots have a mission-first approach and are meticulous about navigating risk. Their mission sets are diverse and changing constantly, hence more risk is concealed. Before every flight, pilots plan their routes, timelines, check their weight and balance, calculate expected fuel burn, file their flight plan, get a weather brief, and much more. Then they complete a Risk Assessment Worksheet outlining the identified risks. Next, they consult with the briefing officer in order to assign a risk value (low, moderate, high, extremely high) to the mission and the flight. A clear commitment to a certain level of risk is made by the pilot and the chain of command before any mission is a "GO."

Once in the air, the Pilot in Command (PC) is the ultimate authority of the aircraft. The PC relies on training and experience to navigate in-flight risks- to always "stay ahead of the aircraft." The PC must think about what the next two to three steps are in the flight, what could go wrong, and what options are available if it does. In an F-35 Lightning Fighter jet with a top speed of about 1200 miles per hour, "staying ahead of the aircraft" is to make multiple decisions in one second before the aircraft travels around 2000 feet or the length of twenty football fields. After the flight comes the learning. The crew conducts an After Action Report (AAR): how the flight went, what went wrong, and what could be improved. Key learnings are then shared with other pilots in the formation. A full cycle of risk navigation – before, during, and after.

You are the Pilot in Command (PC) who should always "stay head of the flight": alert and relevant.

John Boyd, a former military strategist and U.S. Air Force colonel, was known as "40-Second Boyd" for his decisiveness and ability to go from situation assessment to quick action. He believed that an entity, whether a person or an organization, that can complete a cycle of Observe-Orient-Decide-Act effectively will have a competitive advantage. Boyd called his approach the OODA loop. The cycle starts with **Observing** to identify the problem or the threat. It continues with an **Orientation** phase that involves reflecting on what has been observed and considering what should be done. Next, is a **Decision** or response plan. Finally, the cycle ends with an **Action** that carries out the decision. Then the cycle begins again and again. The idea is to be mentally prepared to act rapidly because you are aware of the situation, the risks, and the consequences. He claimed following an OODA loop allows you to get inside the decision cycle of your competitor and tilt the probabilities in your favor.

Great entrepreneurs approach life and business with military precision. They are constantly aiming to "get inside" the competitor's decision cycles. When it comes to accessing risk and learning, be meticulous and observant.

Tim Cook, the CEO of Apple, is most similar to a commercial pilot, focused on meeting investor expectations and steadily steering the ship. In comparison, Steve Jobs could be considered a fighter pilot (maybe even an astronaut), with a cause and a mission to innovate. Bill Gates, the legendary founder of Microsoft, appears to have started as a fighter pilot and then transitioned to a commercial pilot. When Steve Ballmer, Gates' right-hand man who took over as CEO, aimed to get back to his fighter pilot days, his adjusted risk profile and his surrounding structures held him back − struggling with corporate biases and execution habits picked up over the years. The recent Microsoft CEO and Ballmer's successor, Satya Nadella, can be considered a fighter pilot; he has ambition and a mission he has found through applications of Artificial Intelligence.

Joe, my favorite Armenian baker, employs his two daughters and his wife of over thirty years. He is most like a commercial pilot. Between his kids, grandkids, and in-laws, he is responsible for providing for nine people. He is an entrepreneur and, as the old saying goes, "kills what he hunts." He has, over the years, managed to mitigate risk by charting his daily flights carefully and consistently. He opens the store at 4:00 a.m. on the dot every day and bakes the same items at the same quantities he knows he can sell to the regular customers. Some who could be considered commercial pilots use trickery to defuse or delay risk by pretending to be a fighter pilot with innovative thinking. Other leaders get entangled with "risk minimization" and fly (operate and execute) in pursuit of this quarter's bonus − they eat off the flesh until the bones are exposed and the only choice is failure (think of Sears' rapid descent into bankruptcy).

You can be a fighter jet pilot at one stage of your career and then choose to become a commercial pilot. In early stages of a company, founders often have to face more risk. As they get their companies to a stable place, some founders may decide to enjoy a more stable flight. Michael Dell, the legendary founder of Dell computers, was a fighter pilot who navigated his company through a great deal of market and execution risk. He took his company from startup to public. He then became a commercial pilot who navigated the company into a more corporate-like environment and within the boundaries of risk, innovation, and execution defined by the public markets. He made a lot of money and enjoyed a lot of fame and success. A few years later, however, he decided to work with some private equity firms to take Dell from being public back to being privately owned. He was a fighter pilot at heart and did not enjoy commercial flights. Some company owners, in later days of their career, become weekend pilots – taking risks on a very limited basis and in very few situations.

You have a choice in how you navigate risk; you decide the type of pilot you want to be and when your transitions from one kind to another best fit your needs, desires, and stage of life. Remember, you are always navigating risk, even when you delegate the flying to the pilot as a passenger.

> *When it comes to risk, you never stop choosing.*
> *"The single clenched fist lifted and ready,*
> *Or the open asking hand held out and waiting.*
> *Choose:*
> *For we meet by one or the other."*
> **—Carl Sandburg, Swedish-American poet**

TIME TO CHOOSE

Your choices define you and your chances. Decide on what kind of a pilot you desire to be, or choose to be a passenger – once or always. Then explore your relationship with risk. Are you an "Avoider", a "Hangar Seeker", a "Neutralizer," or a "Thrill Chaser?" Make a conscious choice and you will enjoy the evolutionary aftermath.

Get stuck in the contemplation twister and suffer the consequences!

Avoiders try to escape from risk. They aim to sidestep uncertainty in life and always optimize for "risk-free" decisions. In their pursuit of "certainty," they favor indecisiveness and delays. Their quest for safe bets often drives them to get caught in the analysis-paralysis trap. It is hard for avoiders to turn change into opportunity. Avoiders are often in love with their sameness and prefer the status quo. They fear that change may bring about a state that is inferior to their current position. Often, they avoid risk in order to delay or dodge change. At times, however, staying on the sidelines may offer less risk exposure and be the path practicing entrepreneurs may take, while they await the next opportunity. Perpetual Avoiders have no place being pilots and are most happy as passengers.

Most corporate executives are **Hangar Seekers**. They are focused on upside/downside calculations. They tend to be risk minimizers and approach situations from classic Return on Investment (ROI) calculation perspectives and legal angles. Their approach is to find the next hangar, where all is safe. In large organizations, risk mitigation is delegated to professional risk managers. The practice creates two opposing groups: those who promote innovation and experimentation on one side (the so-called intrapreneurs) and those who come up with rules and legalese to guide the company back to safety. Hangar Seekers are constantly searching for ways to protect themselves from exposure to risk and when possible, look to cover their backs by pushing risk decisions onto others – making them more of risk shifters than navigators.

Late in 2011, I entered into a negotiation with KPMG, the global advisory firm with over 200,000 employees, to sell them one of my companies (Wise Window, Inc.). During the due diligence process, I was asked to meet with the head of risk for KPMG. He started the conversation by saying, "You guys are entrepreneurs and risk takers; how do you think you and your team will fit in our organization?" I responded, "We are risk navigators and not risk takers; those guys are in Las Vegas. We invest our own money and every decision is very personal. When we fail, we lose our own money. When you guys make a bad decision, the losses don't impact you and your families."

Fast forward, we did the deal. A couple of years later, as a managing director of the firm I was asked to participate in a "risk management" call designed to evaluate the risks involved with a proposed client agreement. After a thirty minute call, all agreed that there were no risks in executing the contract. All is a "go," the group proclaimed. I had to disagree, by raising a point regarding implied client expectations and termination consequences that no one had considered — a risk that the group was not familiar with! It was a risk that was not in their normal "risk management" playbook. The team of risk experts was trained to look within the boundaries of its harbor and seek safety. But the risks I saw in the agreement were beyond the set of possibilities they had seen before and, therefore, went undetected. The group agreed on amending the agreement. Later, the deal was done and the risk was navigated.

As an observer from the sidelines (risk managers don't execute), you will have a limited ability to identify new risk sources. As a player, a practicing entrepreneur, you have a higher likelihood to see risk approaching...if you remain alert!

Neutralizers are constantly navigating risk in order to defuse it. Risk neutralizers focus on wins, probabilities, and alternative opportunities. Warren Buffet suggests that "risk comes from not knowing what you're doing." Neutralizers are true "navigators." They are in constant risk discovery mode, always trying to understand the probability of occurrence.

Great entrepreneurs are Neutralizers. These entrepreneurs are risk mitigators, stabilizers, and self-directed managers. They look within themselves for regulating decisions based on risk and probabilities and look outside for empirical confirmation or insightful leading signals. Skilled entrepreneurs navigate risk by making less than perfect decisions and avoid the horror of indecision and stagnation. Talented entrepreneurs make decisions in the face of uncertainty – they bet on probabilities. Being a Neutralizer is at the heart of being a practicing entrepreneur. **Navigate the risk and neutralize it.**

According to the FAA, one of the main reasons pilots become accident-prone is their "thrill chasing and adventure seeking" personalities. A **Thrill Chaser** is a pilot who plans for failure. Similarly, entrepreneurs who believe entrepreneurship is about risk-taking as opposed to risk navigation fall into the category of Thrill Chasers. They are individuals who chase the new shiny objects at all times and justify it as being innovative. When faced with competitive challenges, thrill chasers frequently rely on luck and even more risk to guide them to safety. Often, when they face challenges, they assert, "I was dealt a bad poker hand; let's lose it fast, so that I can get the next hand and explore my luck." At times, these individuals indeed get lucky, but the probability is never in their favor – just like at a casino!

Being an entrepreneur is much more than having an idea and an appetite for risk. It is also not about being or getting lucky.

As an entrepreneur, you have to build a PEP that shapes your aviation role in business and in life: a filtering system that can help you realize the risks, assess the probability of occurrence, evaluate the possible consequences, formulate a mitigating plan, and navigate your business towards an evolved position. A unique risk-sensitive operating system that is perfectly tuned to who you are and where you fit along the entrepreneurship gamut. A personalized planning and execution operating platform that helps you accept, circumvent, exploit, transfer, or share the risks you face – the PEP that guides you on how to navigate risk in different situations and become a successful Neutralizer.

Pilots and entrepreneur navigators know that, when it comes to navigating risk, it all depends on the situation. Remember, risk is the bridge that connects today to a different tomorrow. Actions are subject to circumstances, probabilities, and expected outcomes. Sometimes you must accept the risk, other times avoid and seek harbor. Sometimes you need to share and transfer and, in other situations, exploit the risk to open new doors. At all times, however, you must aim to navigate and neutralize risk.

---<>---

But **THERE IS MORE TO BEING A PILOT**, and a lot more to the art and science of entrepreneurship.

Pilots also ignite, fuel, and illuminate. Entrepreneurs face and create choices. They connect, provide, and lead. There is more to entrepreneurship than risk.

CHAPTER ELEVEN:

THERE IS MORE TO BEING A "PILOT!"

Entrepreneurship is the science of uncertainty, risk, and probability and the art of innovation, collaboration, leadership, and choice guided by common sense and stick-to-itiveness.

---<>---

Research indicates that, as adults, we make roughly 35,000 decisions a day. Risk is at the core of every decision we make and it impacts every outcome. Most important decisions have a ripple effect of consequences, choices that compound and can lead to a constant accumulation of risk.

The ability to choose is an incredible and exciting power that influences who you are and what you can become. Regardless of the nature of your decisions, before you choose, don't wait for certainty. If you delay decisions anticipating certainty, you will compromise your future. Don't confuse uncertainty with risk — there will always be unknowns. That doesn't mean it is risky. Good "decisions" are made when risk is neutralized to the extent possible. However, great entrepreneurial decisions are shaped when uncertainty is woven into every action and reaction. Good choices appear when courage blooms and movement is initiated. Great choices appear when the science of entrepreneurship is balanced with the art of innovation, collaboration, leadership, and choice guided by common sense and stick-to-itiveness.

There is more to being an entrepreneur than navigating risk like a pilot. There is also more to being a pilot!

While aviation pilots navigate risk in the sky, maritime pilots are sailors who maneuver ships through dangerous or congested waters. They are navigational experts possessing knowledge of the particular waterway such as its depth, currents, and weather patterns. Maritime pilots are navigators, guides, and leaders. Similarly, an entrepreneur must be able to navigate competitive waters and provide leadership and guidance to others. In the world of trains, a "pilotman" is a railway worker who ensures trains don't collide. The pilotman mitigates risk by maintaining order and keeping a system that shapes movement and activities. An entrepreneur must be able to execute and keep the train moving safely while they innovate and build their company's next best version.

An entrepreneurial pilot is also a light: a flame that is always on and ready to serve as an ignition source. Dedicated entrepreneurs are always ready to fire up their teams with ideas, motivation, and leadership. Moreover, a TV pilot is an experiment, a small-scale preliminary study and a test run for a series – a purposeful activity that is designed to prove an idea. To pilot is to experiment and to reduce risk while thinking big and exploring for more. As an entrepreneur you must act like a pilot and a flame that provides the fuel for the organization to experiment and discover new horizons.

When you choose to be a pilot, you stand ready to provide the initial flame and the fueling energy critical for innovation and experimentation. When you choose to be a pilot you choose to navigate risk by being aware of uncertainties and flexible in actions, while continuously executing against a worthy mission with discipline.

---<>---

You may be a great risk navigator and pilot entrepreneur. You may choose to be the spark that ignites movement and experiments. You may choose to be that flame that sheds light on the jagged road ahead. **But all of that is simply not enough!**

> *"The parts of me that used to think*
> *I was different or smarter or whatever,*
> *almost made me die."*
> **—David Foster Wallace, American author**

At its core, entrepreneurship is about exchange – an exchange of value with others, with the emphasis on others! Entrepreneurial success can only truly crystalize in a thriving ecosystem. A system of interactive and always compounding choices and decisions. An ocean-like connected environment that you shape in order to conceive, create, and deliver value to others in exchange for something of more value to you – satisfying the essence of entrepreneurship.

---<>---

Next, be more than a pilot, more than yourself. Regardless of where you fit on the entrepreneurial gamut, you operate within a self-defined ocean!

Learn to **BE AN OCEAN** and tap into your own unique Oceanness.

CHAPTER TWELVE:

BE AN OCEAN

Unless your intent is to conceive your own products or services, build and deliver them by yourself, and then buy and consume them alone, you must play to win within an ecosystem. Your ecosystem is the environment that defines your interactions, relationships, and the scope of your discoveries. The network of people, systems, behaviors, and connections that allows your entrepreneurial talent to crystalize and be applied in your own unique way. An evolving environment that also defines the edges of your journey as a pilot and a risk navigator.

Your journey is not towards an existing ocean; it is a voyage of knowledge and learning chartered to discover your own supportive ecosystem. As you discover the dimensions of your "Oceanness," you identify characteristics that define this supportive environment. As you navigate the waters of your Oceanness, you continue to shape your Personal Entrepreneurial Philosophy (PEP).

"I need the sea, because it teaches me..."
—Pablo Neruda, Chilean poet and diplomat

To be an ocean is to be dynamic, fluid, and flexible – to find ways around obstacles and competitive forces. It is to be filled with energy and generate power and movement – innovate constantly, move people to excel, and energize customers and markets to grow with you. To be an ocean is to exert your power by being calm and gentle or forceful and deadly. It is to be feared and respected by competitors for your ability to innovate, execute, and compete. It is to be a provider – the builder of a giving ecosystem, a desirable place for employees, customers, investors, and partners to live and thrive. In life, as in entrepreneurship, your Oceanness defines the outer limits of your influence and the strength of your inner circle of relationships.

To be an ocean is to create and exert your Oceanness regardless of where you play and regardless of your origin and limitations.

Like it or not, you live in an ecosystem. Choose to define the Oceanness that works to your advantage or be the victim of randomness. You can define the boundaries of your ocean, regardless of your external environment, the size of your enterprise, what you buy or sell, and to whom you sell. Your Oceanness is the ocean-like qualities that you choose to adhere to, whether your playground is more like a landlocked lake or a river. Regardless of your choice, regardless of where you play, you can be an ocean, a powerful, loved, and feared provider, by creating and exerting your Oceanness.

Whether you manage a small donut shop or are the executive of a healthcare conglomerate focused on fighting diabetes, when it comes to your ecosystem, you have the same set of mental forces at your disposal. Size does not matter, but attitude does. Adopting the characteristics of an ocean as you shape your entrepreneurial philosophy has nothing to do with the magnitude of your organization or the vastness of your dreams. In any business, money is invested, customers are needed, employees build the culture, and suppliers and partners support execution. Every individual lives in an ecosystem and every business operates in an ecosystem. Your ecosystem can be two people or two hundred thousand people.

What is relevant is how and
to what extent you choose
to embrace the spirit of the ocean.
The spirit of being a provider,
a connector, and an energizer
that can give life, but also
destroy and renew!

---<>---

THE PROVIDER

The ocean is where life began and it remains home to the majority of Earth's plants and animals, from tiny single-celled organisms to the planet's largest living animal, the blue whale. The ocean contains more species per square meter than any other natural ecosystem in the world. There are currently over one million identified species that live in the ocean, and scientists agree that countless more exist that have not yet been named or identified. The ocean holds considerable unknowns, mysteries that hold amazing promises.

The ocean is a self-sustaining ecosystem with a balanced food chain: an environment where energy and nutrients are passed from one organism to another. It is a place where all inhabitants can feed, procreate, and grow. An environment where balance is not translated to equal distribution, but efficient, appropriate, and timely allocation. The ocean is an ecosystem where constant exchange of value and life between its denizens is the daily norm.

Oceans drive change while protecting the order.

As the sun's trusted partner, oceans absorb ninety-eight percent of its radiation. Oceans drive the global weather patterns as they transfer the heat to the atmosphere. They provide over seventy percent of the oxygen we breathe and over ninety-seven percent of the world's water supply while constantly under attack by natural sources and manmade pollution. Every minute, oceans offer a never-ending supply of energy by forming waves: the energy that fuels progress, change, and livelihood for all.

To be an ocean is to be a provider to all that you come in contact with. It is to embrace the unknown and appreciate the undiscovered. It is to give life, to sustain life, and to shape life. To be an ocean is to be resilient, patient, and peaceful while holding the power to unleash anger at will and destroy opposition.

Your Oceanness reflects the intensity of your choice to learn from the ocean, to behave like an ocean and to make its qualities your own.

THE CONNECTOR

An ecosystem is dependent upon connections and reciprocity. Often, the survival and growth of one species is directly connected to that of another. Being a provider is more than selling a product to your customers, giving a paycheck to your employees, or placing an order with your suppliers. An entrepreneurial ecosystem (ocean) reaches beyond customers and employees. It includes those who are invested in the company and, in the case of public companies, those analysts who put a price on the stock. Those who supply products and services are also a part of the ecosystem. Most critically, the entrepreneurs' and employees' family members are a part, too. As an entrepreneur, your ocean should be designed to provide for all species within it, whether directly or indirectly. All species are equally entitled to receive value.

A provider is also a connector, a builder, a promoter, and a trusted friend. The provider facilitates the creation of a network of value to all involved. As you define the dimensions of your Oceanness, you define the extent of the value you are willing to deliver to all those within your ocean. As a provider, you must lead and motivate others to continually look to the depth of the unknown and discover new value. In other words, innovate. Beyond people and activities, you must help connect ideas and opportunities, turn chaos and storms into calmness and beauty, and aim to reestablish balance over and over. As you form your Oceanness, you will discover the real you.

"Just imagine becoming the way you used to be as a very young child,
before you understood the meaning of any word,
before opinions took over your mind.
The real you is loving, joyful, and free.
The real you is just like a flower,
just like the wind, just like the ocean..."
—Don Miguel Ruiz, Mexican author

Robert owns a small, but thriving telecommunications distribution business. He offers prepaid calling cards as well as internet and cable services online and through independent retailers. Besides providing the customers the best relevant product selections, prices and service, he is also a provider to the rest of his ecosystem. When a supplier was struggling in her business, he tapped into his network to find her new customers. When he learned that one of his field representatives had an issue with his wife's car and that she was struggling to get the kids to school because her automobile insurer was being difficult and not paying her claim after an accident, he restructured his employee's compensation plan to help him make some quick cash to secure reliable transportation for his kids. When he learned that some of the retailers had a difficult time with customer traction and foot traffic, he offered his team's search and Search Engine Optimization (SEO) capabilities to help — not only selling his company's products but also helping retailers to increase sales of the other products they offered. He also used his know-how to help his telco providers identify online black-market players who were causing considerable operational and brand erosion headaches. Robert aimed to be a provider and a connector to all in his ecosystem.

Make every drop of your ocean count.

To be a provider, you have to be a connector. To be a connector, you have to be aware of the connection points and the moments of interaction. A provider is in tune with the needs of the ecosystem and aims to create the connections and circumstances to satisfy those needs. As a provider, you are not responsible to satisfy all needs. You are, however, expected to help create an environment wherein needs can be satisfied. For a practicing entrepreneur and provider, every connection and action matters. The ocean is a collection of small drops of water: a collection of connections, values, and interactions. As you define your ocean and shape your Oceanness, value everyone and every interaction. Every drop within the ocean matters. Collectively, they make up who you are and what you can achieve.

"We ourselves feel that what we are doing is just
a drop in the ocean.
But the ocean would be less because of that missing drop."
-Mother Teresa, Albanian-Indian
Roman Catholic nun and missionary

---<>---

THE ENERGIZER

You shape your own best version within the boundaries of your ecosystem. If you choose to adopt ocean-like characteristics, you have three energy-generating wave-like forces at your disposal.

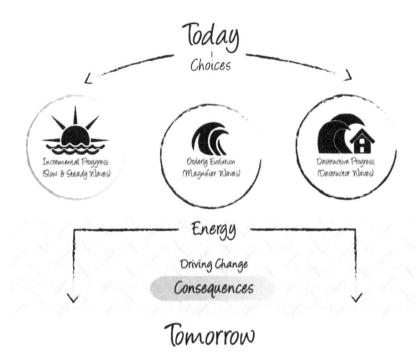

i) The **slow and steady waves** that ensure incremental progress and help you build your organization's culture.

ii) The **magnifier waves** which are often caused by external markets and major customer movements. Waves that generate massive energies and forces that, if captured in time and effectively directed, can help you evolve in an orderly fashion. If ignored, these waves can be detrimental.

iii) The **destructor waves (tsunamis)** generate the maximum force. They are caused by major innovations and market dynamics – the creation of cars, personal computers, smart phones, internet-based commerce, Viagra, Artificial Intelligence, etc. For some, these waves are destructive. They cause bankruptcies and, for many, irreversible demise

(Blockbuster, Kodak, and Sears). For others, they offer fame and fortune (Apple, Microsoft, Amazon, Pfizer, and Ford).

No sea is always calm and no storm is forever. Practicing entrepreneurs with well-developed PEPs are always prepared to take advantage of the forces at their disposal to push their cause forward. The energies generated from the different wave-like forces complement each other as they help entrepreneurs navigate their organizations. Practicing entrepreneurs realize that every movement matters, that every means is an end to itself, and every action and reaction defines who they are and who they can become.

> *"The least movement is of importance to all nature.*
> *The entire ocean is affected by a pebble."*
> **— Blaise Pascal, 17th century French mathematician,**
> **Inventor, and theologian**

The Slow and Steady

Ocean waves are powerful forces that erode and shape the world's coastlines. Partnering with the wind, the ocean constantly generates energy through small waves, creating wave trains or a collection of connected small ripples that can, over time, get bigger and more forceful. Winds that blow over the top of the ocean create friction between the air and water molecules, creating a frictional drag that shows up as waves on the surface of the ocean. The slow and mostly steady wind waves offer the energy for the ocean to remain fluid and dynamic. They offer the constant energy needed to grow and provide. These waves slowly reshape the shorelines and smooth the rough surfaces of headlands.

In business, slow and steady waves are generated by the winds produced by normal and constant change in business dynamics: market demand and supply, functional product improvements, performance adjustments by both you and your competitors, etc.

These winds offer the force needed for waves of growth and forward movement to gain energy; these are waves that help your business remain in motion and follow a path of steady and often predictable evolution. This is the energy that runs the day-to-day business.

Ocean water is always in motion, but ocean waves do not necessarily represent a flow of water. While slow and steady waves transport energy over great distances, only a small amount of water within them actually moves in a horizontal direction. Instead, the water moves vertically. This is why a buoy set out in the middle of an ocean moves up and down, but does not travel far. An entrepreneur who behaves like an ocean is able to transfer the energy of normal business winds to all within their ecosystem. The energy that propels the organization to create, build, and deliver while enjoying a constant culture and execution rhythm. An organization that is fully energized and dynamic while staying in place, together, and connected.

As an organization, or as an individual, be like a buoy - in motion, but steady.

The Magnifiers

Ocean swells are created by major tropical storms – these are the magnifier waves. Think of major external forces that impact your life and business (e.g., business model shifts, tariffs, technological advancements, and digital transformation in business or a divorce and a new baby in your personal life). They are large enough forces that can have significant effects on your organization and life, but are a lot less lethal than destructor energies. Entrepreneurial swells often begin with shifts in customer expectations (e.g., emphasis on experience) or super efficiency boosters (e.g., faster computers or more capable software). They slowly gain momentum as needs are better defined and served and/or as technologies are used more widely across the industry.

Magnifier waves provide the energy for a more orderly evolution process. They do not approach as suddenly as deadly tsunamis and are more predictable. However, they offer an opportunity for the innovators and change makers to put some distance between themselves and the competitors. These are waves that can help magnify your competitive advantages.

Always, stay alert of the magnifying waves, ride them.
Use their energy to advance your cause.

When Amazon used technology and robots to improve online conversion or logistics operations, the slow and steady waves were in play. When it acquired Whole Foods and connected the online/offline grocery business, Amazon responded to customer expectations for freshness and local delivery and were able to ride a magnifying business wave. When Amazon created Kindle (the electronic book tablet) or Alexa (the smart speaker that listens to voice commands) and when it disrupted the book business with e-commerce, it created a Tsunami – a destructive force for others but a constructive force for Amazon.

The Destructors

Harbor waves or tsunamis are waves that are shaped by an abrupt disturbance underwater (e.g., volcanic eruption, landslide, or even a nuclear explosion). The most common cause of a tsunami is an earthquake. Tsunami waves that begin in the deep and vast oceans have a very small wave height. However, they move fast and can be very wide, spanning more than 1,000 football fields across. As the tsunami approaches the coastline and shallow water, it slows in speed, but builds in height. When the tsunami comes ashore, it brings with it a tremendous amount of energy – waves as high as 100 feet. Tsunamis can deliver pure destruction. They also bring an opportunity to rebuild.

In business, a tsunami is a major life-changing event – new technologies eliminating the old approaches (e.g., streaming music replacing CDs), natural causes (COVID-19) instigating mass behavioral changes, or innovations making your value proposition obsolete. While some companies become the victims of tsunamis and vanish, other companies create their own destinies by being innovators (not leaving change to chance). Some business tsunamis are induced internally. When Steve Ballmer left Microsoft in 2014 and Satya Nadella took over as CEO, the massive beast of Microsoft moved towards its next more improved version by the force of a tsunami – causing close to a fourfold increase in the company's capitalization. Nadella engineered the tsunami and delivered the force of change he called a "refresh" through reshuffling the company's vision, heavily embracing artificial intelligence, and revising how Microsoft sells and delivers products or collaborates with others (e.g., One Commercial Partner Model). Recently, IBM replaced its CEO with an Indian-born, cloud computing executive. After years of stagnation and struggling to evolve, the company hopes that it can replicate the success that Nadella brought to Microsoft. IBM's apparent imitation is not a tsunami. Where you were born, your education, or your previous corporate experience does not guarantee your ability to be able to create a tsunami. Your Oceanness and your PEP fuel that ability. Always remember: You Are NOT Them!

When faced with a tsunami, we can either press on with our old beliefs and approaches and aim to ride the same old waves or use the force of the tsunami to our advantage. Steve Jobs returned to Apple in 1997 after a period of exile. Roughly a decade later, he created a tsunami with the force of one product, the iPod. The first smartphone was introduced by BlackBerry in 1999. Eight years later, Jobs' next big move was the iPhone – a device that pushed the limits of usability and interactivity considerably forward. BlackBerry, which ruled the smartphone market at one point with more than a fifty percent market share, had a zero percent share after rounding (actually 0.0004827) by 2017. The reaction of Samsung, however, was entirely different. The first Samsung smartphone was introduced two years after the iPhone (in 2009). As of April 2019, Statcounter reports that Samsung controls about thirty-one percent of the mobile vendor market share worldwide and Apple sits closer to twenty-three percent.

All tsunamis are destructive, unless you direct the force towards your advantage. They are destructive, but can also be vehicles that you can use to your advantage.

Not all tsunamis start as one. Some begin with an attitude, a gesture, or a slow and steady wave. Some tropical waves can turn into market changing tsunamis that can be destructive to some and delightfully constructive for others. By redefining the coffee experience, Starbucks forever changed the retail coffee business. It created a third space (besides home and work) for customers and delivered a consistent experience while allowing patrons to create their own coffee drinks. It leveraged the magnifying wave of changing customer expectations to shape a global tsunami over time.

Jack Taylor, a former used car salesman who never graduated from college, decided to compete with the giants of the car rental business in 1957. Enterprise Rent-A-Car started with seventeen cars and today, as a primarily family-owned business, has a market valuation (according to Warren Buffet) that far exceeds Avis and Hertz. The slow, but growing, wave of change Enterprise started was rooted in customer satisfaction. By 2008, Enterprise ranked twenty-first on the 2008 Forbes list of "Largest Private Companies in America." The force that mobilized the initial tropical storm in the industry was the focus on local rental car markets – rentals for people who needed a replacement car after an accident, mechanical repair, theft, or for a special occasion. Thirty-five years after Taylor started, he expanded the business to the airport market, where all other rental companies had been very active for years. Early in the 21st century, *Business Week* placed Enterprise on the top ten list of places to launch a career. In the case of Enterprise, there was no magical technology, but there was an undiscovered value proposition that became the force behind the tsunami. The growth was ignited by the company's focus on customers, paying attention to a sector of the market that had not been well-served, and providing employees with a tremendous opportunity to grow. When Taylor started the company, Avis and Hertz were already conglomerates with thousands of cars in their fleets. These competitors continued on their previously chosen path; they were not destroyed by the tsunami and stayed successful for years by most accounts. But it can be argued that they did not take advantage of the tsunami of change that Enterprise created in order to realize their own true potential. Amid the COVID-19 pandemic, Enterprise is positioned to expand its fifty-seven percent market share (including other owned brands) while Hertz has filed for bankruptcy.

Watch out for advantageous waves generated by competitors, markets, or crises and choose to ride them. Consider turning them into your manufactured tsunamis. Some tsunamis are triggered by external crises and shaped through your responses. In 2020, the world was crippled by a deadly, invisible virus. The news of the future was filled with doom and gloom.

In the depths of darkness, however, the flip side to this crisis was evolving every day. The hopeful side. The innovative side. The side that rewards creativity and collaboration. The opportunity that is controlled by the mother of all inventions: necessity. As chaos, confusion, and peril loomed over the globe, old and new innovations appeared as remedies. Faced with the consequences of COVID-19, the world forcefully pushed past various innovation resistance lines, lines that when crossed changed our lives forever. Old initiatives like e-commerce, telehealth, and distance learning led the massive change initiatives. People across various ages, ethnicities, religious, and political beliefs overcame their addictions to sameness and fear of change. Masses at an unprecedented speed overcame their opposition to using technology, working from home, trusting the web with their banking needs, clicking to buy groceries, and attending happy hour through their phones. People across the globe crossed resistance lines on their way to a "contact-free but connection-filled economy" where digital and invisible bridges connect people and things from many directions. Although the clear, long-term winners shaped by this tsunami are still not yet declared, some front runners are appearing: Amazon and Zoom. Entrepreneurs and organizations who are willing and able to use this tsunami to their advantage will be rewarded. Those are the entrepreneurs who actuate their mindfulness and direct their wanderlust.

Warning: Put your entire focus on creating a tsunami all the time and you will likely lose the steady energy critical to staying a viable business. Let the magnifier waves derail you and you will put your business at risk. For optimal effect, the waves and the energies must be leveraged strategically and in balance.

Your ocean is a collection of drops; each important, each valuable, each an ocean itself.

"You are not a drop in the ocean.
You are the entire ocean in a drop."
—Jalâluddîn Rumi, 13th century poet
and metaphysicist

Next, discover and acknowledge **THE OCEAN WITHIN.**

CHAPTER THIRTEEN:

THE OCEAN WITHIN

While convincing my parents to let me emigrate to the U.S. from Iran at the age of 16, I used the words of my grandfather when he started his own journey to a bigger city close to 100 years ago: "Small fish grow in small waters; big fish grow in the ocean." Over the years, I have learned that it is neither the vastness of the land that defines your growth, nor your placement in the ocean that secures your success. It is your ability to place the ocean inside your thoughts and behavior and become a dynamic provider who embraces change and turns movement and friction into waves of energy that fuel success. I learned that you need to become an ocean before you can become a big fish! To discover lasting treasures, there is no place to swim to but within.

"I do not know what I may appear to the world;
but to myself, I seem to have been only like a boy
playing on the seashore,
and diverting myself now and then
in finding a smoother pebble
or prettier shell than ordinary,
while the great ocean of truth
lay all undiscovered before me."
—Isaac Newton, English physicist, astronomer, and theologian

Your best version is always hidden somewhere in your ocean, waiting to be discovered and improved by your Oceanness. Being an ocean is a state of mind; it's what you need to "be" in order to fuel your entrepreneurial talents and transition from the denial stage to aspirational and practicing.

The choices you make around your Oceanness are critical when personalizing your entrepreneurial philosophy. You can choose to be a harbor seeker, anchored to the safety of the past you know, or set sail towards the unknown, capture the wind of knowledge, remain fluid, and become a provider: become one with the ocean. A drop with all the potential of an ocean and an ocean with all the capabilities and powers of all the drops put together.

*"You can either see yourself as a wave in the ocean
or you can see yourself as the ocean."*
**—Oprah Winfrey, American talk show host, producer,
actress, author, and philanthropist**

You are not them. Choose well based on who you are and you will thrive through the strength of your unique brand of entrepreneurship. Aim to copy what has made others successful, or rely on "how-to" rules, and you will compromise your originality and true potential.

---<>---

As you explore the ocean within, **BE YOU. BE AUTHENTIC.**

Next, navigate through the jagged paths ahead as you purposefully apply your innate wanderlust and shape your journey to discover your originality.

Let your Oceanness be guided only by the authentic you. Let it shape situations, choices, and consequences. Let it shape the leader in you and the forever evolving sculpture of you.

CHAPTER FOURTEEN:

BE YOU ... THE AUTHENTIC YOU

Your entrepreneurial spirit is like a river. Get out of its way and let it flow through you. Let it fall into your ocean and shape your Oceanness. Trust your ability to pilot your aircraft and land in opportunities, always. Rely on your unique Oceanness and your adeptness to dance with life and the consequences and stay relevant. Then, lead the way to prosperity in your own unique way. Leadership is a quality that fuels progress and ignites purposeful change. Leadership is the engine of entrepreneurship. Warren Bennis, the American scholar and author, puts it best: "Leadership is the capacity to translate vision into reality." The vision of you and the reality of your future. Aim to be only superior to your former self – evolve authentically.

"There is nothing noble in being superior to your fellow man; true nobility is being superior to your former self."
—Ernest Hemingway, American writer

In the game of golf, how you swing the club at the golf ball drives the magic of winning games. Legend has it that all players have an authentic swing in them and that great players have the ability to find the swing within, the authentic swing that makes the player legendary and unforgettable! Discover and fine-tune your own authentic leadership swing. The perfect swing that drives the perfect entrepreneurial game.

*"Inside each and every one of us is one true authentic swing...
Somethin' we was born with... Somethin' that's ours and ours alone...
Somethin' that can't be taught to ya or learned...
Somethin' that got to be remembered...
Over time the world can, rob us of that swing...
It get buried inside us under
all our wouldas and couldas and shouldas..."*
—The Legend of Bagger Vance

To be "you" is not about blind acceptance of incompetence or being delusional about your greatness. It is about a developing and evolving confidence and not intolerable arrogance. It is about knowing and wisdom. It is about discovery of your hidden talents. You have the capacity to lead, to excel, and to author your next best version. Be you. Accept that you are an entrepreneur, a leader, and a sculptor.

To lead your own unique way is to be prepared to constantly define and redefine yourself. Constantly define your awesomeness and failures. To stand ready to redefine your abilities and scope of influence. To redraw the boundaries of your leadership and expectations based on situations. Do what you must, and not just what you can; that is how you push the limits of your abilities and evolve.

Listen and learn, but never take the bait and try to imitate someone else. Sandra Day O'Connor, the first female U.S. Supreme Court justice, claims that by watching her mother she learned an important lesson that would guide her through life: "Don't take the bait." A key step towards losing yourself is to "take the bait" and strive to be an imitation of someone else. Worse is to fall into the trap of impersonating a shadow- an imaginary self-portrait modeled after a delusion.

Lead and build as YOU, the dynamic and evolving YOU.
Because what you build is who you are and who you are is what you build!

---<>---

We are all innate leaders. Leadership is the twin brother of entrepreneurship – the face most visible to others. All leaders are entrepreneurs and all entrepreneurs have the talent to lead. As entrepreneurs facing uncertainty, seek to exchange your current position with an improved one. Swim out to gain knowledge and create something new and more valuable.

To be authentic is to realize that as a leader your job is neither to impart greatness on people, nor to implant greatness within them. John Quincy Adams, the sixth U.S. president, said: "If your actions inspire others to dream more, learn more, do more and become more, you are a leader." The founder of philosophical Taoism, Lao Tzu, believed that an authentic leader is at their best "when people barely know he exists, when his work is done, his aim fulfilled, they will say: we did it ourselves." Be effective, but transparent.

Lead or be led, that is your choice. Be mindful of situations, because good leadership is not all about leading at all times, but to lead at the right time and follow when necessary.

Be authentic whether you choose to lead or follow.

"Be yourself, everyone else is already taken."
—Oscar Wilde, 19th century
Irish poet and playwright

When it comes to life, entrepreneurship and leadership you have an **AXIOM OF CHOICES**.

Next, explore your choices and stand ready to shape your unique brand of leadership. Leadership that fits the authentic you and the situations you face.

CHAPTER FIFTEEN:
AXIOM OF CHOICES

The domain and scope of leadership is situational and different for everyone. However, leadership effectiveness is impacted by some universal principles, dynamic tenets which guide leaders to excel across circumstances. Principles that fit together like Legos to shape your leadership style and are foundational to your PEP. Vital factors that are rooted in trust, awareness, communication, competency, and courage. Imperatives that, when claimed and owned by the authentic you, will shape your wisdom and your wins. Everyone owns his or her unique past and faces a distinct future. To be you is to embrace your originality, regardless of your origins. It is creating the conditions of success, over and over.

Your unique and original leadership style is shaped by five dynamic but controllable elements. The essential axiom of your choices: the self-evident truths that require no proof. Universal principles that are also pillars of your PEP. A collection of tenets that apply to all leadership situations but never in the same proportions. Your axiom of choices offers avenues to express your genius.

"Because genius is a characteristic of consciousness,
genius is also universal.
That which is universal is, therefore,
theoretically available to every man.
It awaits only the right circumstances to express it."
—Sir David Hawkins, MD, PhD, psychiatrist, physician,
researcher, and spiritual teacher

On this journey, lead like yourself and no one else. As you lead, choose your actions and preferences from the axiom of choices.

Based on situations, choose from a continuum of beliefs, behaviors, and options. How you make choices is how you define your leadership one choice at a time. There are five dynamic principles you can use to navigate through possibilities. They offer a menu of choices for you to shape your own leadership style. The first tenet is focused around *"Three Way Trust"* – trust them, help them trust you, and work on trusting yourself. The second tenet is *"Variable Communication"* – to be effective you must be understood. The third tenet is *"Overarching Courage"* – the quality of mind or spirit that enables you to face difficulty and overcome fear. The fourth tenet is *"Situational Awareness"* – the ability to fit your talents to circumstances. The fifth tenet is *"Constant Competency"* – that incompetent leaders are inferior competitors.

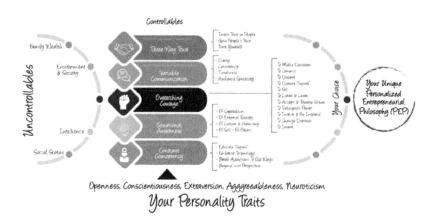

FIRST TENET: THREE WAY TRUST

> *"He who does not trust enough, will not be trusted."*
> **—Lao Tzu, Chinese philosopher**

Trust is at the very core of leadership. It is the glue that fuses all relationships together. People follow you if they trust you. You may lead because you are the boss, because they fear you, or because they need the job. However, for the troops to follow you into a minefield of unknowns and into the battlefield of innovation and competition, they need to trust you, your vision, and your convictions. For followers to unleash their amazing powers of creativity and apply their intellectual muscles to make your vision a reality, you must capture their hearts and minds. But, before they trust you, you must first trust them. Reciprocal trust is a preciously earned investment. As you invest in them and they invest in you, the compounded returns create an amazing force of courage and creativity. Ernest Hemingway suggested, as a starting point, "The best way to find out if you can trust somebody is to trust them."

After you invest trust in others and then gain their trust in return, there is a third trust that influences leadership – the trust you invest in yourself. To trust yourself, you must first be convinced of your worthiness. Gaining confidence is an iterative process in which you repeatedly challenge your assumptions and conclusions and gain more confidence. To trust yourself is not to be bullheaded about your thoughts or attempt to tackle tasks despite obvious inabilities. It is to be comfortable accepting opposing views and knowing that your ideas can be improved. A self-trust that, if not honest and genuine, shatters the trust of others in you.

**Choose to trust yourself and others
and you have gained access
to the most effective tool of leadership:
their trust in you.**

SECOND TENET: VARIABLE COMMUNICATIONS

A critical pillar of effective communications is *clarity*. Illusive communications lead to illusive results. Period. Clarity of communication is directly related to your clarity of thought, which stems from your PEP.

> *"The single biggest problem in communication is*
> *the illusion that it has taken place."*
> **—George Bernard Shaw,**
> **Irish playwright and political activist**

Another key pillar is *consistency* expressed through your words and deeds. Clarity without consistency leads to confusion. Effective communication occurs when the information communicated connects the audience to the past, the present, and the future, providing a road map of progression. Your audience truly comprehends when the communication is placed in the context of existing understanding; it is framed with the parameters and conditions of today and it points to an outcome that is different in the future. Context matters. Always relate the communication to the situation that you are in. Inconsistent communication breaks the continuity of expectations and negatively impacts trust. Be inconsistent in what you say and what you do, and expect erratic outcomes. Be inconsistent with what you say today versus yesterday, without clear justification, and you erode trust.

Your message must resonate with variability but never be inconsistent.

Other dimensions of variable communications include *timeliness* and *audience sensitivity*. In terms of timeliness, delay what you must communicate or be too early and you lose effectiveness. If you deliver the medicine too early, the drug may be toxic; deliver it too late, and the patient may die. Equally important is audience sensitivity. If you speak the same to all, you face incomprehension. Use language, tone, and content that is relevant and appropriate to your audience. Otherwise, you will simply "fail to communicate." Your message is important but what they hear is much more important. Under all situations, get to the message before your audience's imagination collapses.

John Maxwell, the leadership guru, claims that, "You are only as good of a leader as others perceive you to be." When it comes to communication, variability is key.

When you choose how to communicate, you choose how your leadership is perceived.

THIRD TENET: OVERARCHING COURAGE

"Courage is the first of human qualities
because it is the quality which guarantees the others."
—Aristotle, Greek philosopher

Courage is an ability to face and push through fear; to bravely act and stand for something. Courage is the force behind movement and agility. It shapes your confidence and fuels your will. It strengthens your determination to respond to change, to shape change, and to make change. Courage empowers you to commit and to dissent as you face uncertainty.

You demonstrate courage every time you decide and take a position, admit to mistakes and learn; relinquish your power to others, and invent or embrace change. You demonstrate courage every time you reshape and reveal your new version – every time you improve the sculpture of you.

Having overarching courage is a sword that can cut both ways. Courageous leaders can choose to build lasting organizations that prosper far beyond their imagination. They can also choose or pave the road to disaster. To be courageous does not make one wise, just, or sensible. Unjust leaders with shallow and deceptive visions can also be resilient and courageous. Effective but misguided leaders like Adolf Hitler, Ayatollah Khomeini and Genghis Khan all applied courage to ill intentions.

Courage is situational, too. A force for good or evil. Be careful how you apply it!

Courage impacts your leadership in different ways:

i) **Courage to make decisions and to commit:** Have the courage to decide between choices. Realize that one hundred percent confidence in decisions is a fool's decree. Play the probability game: avoid indecisiveness rooted in uncertainty. Commit to deadlines, to products, to missions, and to causes. The results you achieve are rooted in your decisions materialized through your commitments.

ii) **Courage to dissent and to dispute thyself:** You have an obligation to yourself and to your organization to dissent. Never consent to actions not aligned with your PEP unless you evolve your philosophy along the way and communicate that evolution. Require data and logic and be aware and wary of emotional decisions rooted in the desire to please others. Be willing to trigger conflict in order to get to a better answer. Dispute thyself and look at situations from various and opposing points of view. To learn, constantly change your frame of reference. To become an improved version of YOU, first question the previous version and aim to enhance it over and over.

iii) **Courage to fail, to listen and learn, and to accept and tolerate:** Missteps and failures are human. Seek opportunities to fail and learn, but never let yourself and your team be content with failure. Acceptance of failure is the first step towards learning, creativity, innovation, change and progress. If you have never failed, you have never tried; you have compromised your future. Missteps only turn into mistakes when we fail to admit them. When we fail to learn from them. Bruce Lee, the martial artist and philosopher, said it best: "Mistakes are always forgivable, if one has the courage to admit them." Your learning begins with your openness to genuinely examine situations and your courage to accept being wrong.

iv) **Courage to relinquish power, to inspire and be inspired:** Don't empower others. Help them unleash their own power and ignite forward movement. Acknowledge that it is they, your employees and partners, who have the ultimate power of creativity and execution. Inspire them to unleash their inherent entrepreneurial and leadership talents. Let them inspire you to elevate your game and see beyond your own limitations. Inspiration must be bilateral and requires courage.

v) **Courage to change direction and to invent:** Billy Graham, the American evangelist, put it best: "Courage is contagious. When a brave man takes a stand, the spines of others are often stiffened." When it is time to change direction and innovate against conventions, be decisive and committed. Be brave enough to take a stand. Have the courage to go a different way; the courage to admit that a previously promising path and focus is no longer a good choice. When you choose to lead, you promise your followers to guide them from one place to a presumably better place. Be ready to innovate in order to fulfill that promise. To innovate, you must be courageous. Your organization must learn to be courageous, too.

The limit of your potential, what you can be tomorrow, is the limit of your ability to be courageous today.

FOURTH TENET: SITUATIONAL AWARENESS

I learned a lesson about the impact of situational awareness during my first year of college, although I did not appreciate its value until years later. My physics professor always came to class wearing a dark suit and tie. He was anything but handsome. He was the target of chuckles and meaningless jokes by the students who mostly showed up in shorts suffering a slight hangover from fraternity parties the night before.

One day, after a half-hour lecture, he turned to the blackboard and folded his suit jacket so you could no longer see his tie. He then turned to the class and asked, "Who can guess the color and the pattern of my tie?" He stated that the first person to guess correctly could skip the class for the rest of the semester. This was clearly quite the carrot!

Hands went up all over the place and a previously silent class suddenly became alert and engaged. Blue, red, yellow, and other random answers came from all corners of the room. The professor then gave Bill, who had his hand up from the first moment, a chance. "Your tie is red with yellow patterns of little birds, almost a couple of inches apart." Bill was dead on!

After some praise, the professor explained. "We all do things for a reason, whether we are conscious of it or not. I woke up this morning and faced a closet full of suits and ties; I picked this tie because I felt cheerful and energetic. This is my favorite tie because my daughter bought it. After months of not seeing her, I will be seeing her for lunch today." Everything we do has a story and a reason. To be aware of your surroundings is the first step in understanding people and situations. A way to get one step closer to reasons and reasonable actions. As a side note, Bill did not take the professor up on his offer and, fully alert, stayed in class for the rest of the semester. He aced the class. I recently heard that he founded a technology company that went public – clearly, being situationally aware pays off!

All situations hold the promise of "great things." To do great things, you must understand the situations you face. To command great things, you must also understand the situations others face. To be an effective leader, you must be fully aware of situations: your capabilities, external realities, cultures, and people.

If you ignore your capabilities (organization or self), and the realities that influence your strategies and execution (the situation), you are erecting a vision on shaky ground; a house of cards that will fall when faced with competitive pressures.

When you lack understanding of others (your employees, customers, partners, teammates, or even family members) and their situations, you introduce an unwarranted risk: that they will lose interest in you and your vision. If they are uninterested, your leadership is compromised.

Culture is shaped when an organization faces new situations, when it drives for performance, when it seeks new growth areas, and when it struggles with operating challenges. Culture is built slowly, one hire and fire at a time, one failure and success at a time- not by committees. Culture is formed at the cross section of leadership and situations. It is both the cause and effect of leadership. It can be the source of harmonious and productive energy as well as the force of disruption and demise.

Choose to be unaware of situations and you choose to compromise your leadership and your future.

Simon Bolivar, "El Libertador," was a Venezuelan soldier and statesman who led the revolution against Spanish rule. Bolívar is regarded, by many, to be the greatest genius the Latin American world has produced. The country of Bolivia was named after him. Simón Bolívar was a trusted man of the people; his words and actions resonated across South America. His vision of freedom and his courage to rise up against the Spanish was adored by millions across a continent. He was a great wartime leader. He failed miserably, however, on almost every front when it came to keeping the union of the parties and governing in post-revolutionary times. When civil wars overcame the joy of independence, the leaders' mistrust of each other destroyed the strength that defeated the Spanish. Faced with a new situation, Bolivar failed the awareness test. The situation around him and thus the capabilities he needed, the motivations required, and the needs of the people, had all changed. He failed to align his leadership with the realities around him. His lack of awareness drove him to irreversible failure.

"To do great things is difficult;
but to command great things is more difficult".
—Friedrich Nietzsche,
German scholar and philosopher

FIFTH TENET: CONSTANT COMPETENCY

Incompetence begins with the assumption of knowledge and sameness. Learn to change and adapt, always. Embrace technology, the tools and tricks of the industry you are in, and the trends that impact your organization and markets. Be in the learning mode constantly. Educate thyself. Continuously reexamine your addictions to past behaviors and biases and break your addictions and adherence to old ways. Welcome change.

As a leader, accept the new and develop a *beyond now* perspective. Let your competency command respect. Incompetence breeds incompetence.

"I am, as I've said, merely competent.
But in an age of incompetence,
that makes me extraordinary."
—Billy Joel, American singer and songwriter

Roberto was the maître d' at an Italian restaurant my partner and I frequented during the 1990s. One night, he approached us while we were in a wine-induced good mood and asked if we could help him with his entrepreneurial dream. We agreed to meet with him the next day, a Saturday. He and his four months pregnant wife arrived at our office around 11:30 a.m. He was a young Iranian man who had moved to Italy a few years after the 1979 Islamic revolution in Iran. He had been in the U.S. for about nine months, and had met and married his wife almost immediately after his arrival in Los Angeles. He captured our imagination within the first fifteen minutes of our meeting with his colorful and enticing description of how to cook a steak and make it instantaneously melt in your mouth. My partner and I were impressed by his ability to make such a simple dish sound so exciting. We both became hungry on the spot!

When he arrived in Italy, Roberto's first job was as a busboy. He was promoted to a waiter and then maître d'. After gaining the trust of the owner and the restaurant's chef, he was admitted into the kitchen. After a few years, he became a sous-chef and then the restaurant's manager before immigrating to America. He had big ambitions and felt America was the place to realize his dream of owning his own restaurant. He had his eye on Malibu and was asking us to help him find a location and negotiate a lease. He was confident that if he had a place, his success would be imminent. We inquired about his finances and he proudly announced that he had almost $3,000. Roberto certainly seemed very competent in his craft. He had filled every position in a restaurant and could certainly get customers hungry with just his descriptions. He was ambitious but naïve, we thought, as we tried to get him to be realistic—work a bit longer and save a bit more before attempting to open a restaurant. To not completely demolish his dreams, we left him with the idea that we would help him if he could find a place within his budget (the chances were slim) or in a year or two when he had a more reasonable initial investment needed.

Two weeks later, Roberto showed up at our office and our receptionist announced his arrival with great enthusiasm. He entered the conference room with a very big smile on his face – he had found a spot that was within his budget: a sandwich shop in a strip mall in Culver City that only served lunch. The place was owned by an elderly Korean couple. The business was in trouble because the major neighborhood employer (Hughes Helicopter) had moved away from the area and the owners just wanted out. He had, with broken English, spoken to them and convinced them to give him a deal: a five-year payment plan of $300 a month. He had used his entire savings of $3,000 as a down payment.

Roberto proved to be highly competent in the restaurant business. He took over immediately and introduced pasta at lunch. His pasta and sandwiches developed a reputation in the neighborhood. At night he would cut and nail the wood pieces he had purchased from Home Depot to build chairs and tables. While his pregnant wife was in charge of the cash register, he was the maître d', the server, the busboy, and the chef, all rolled into one. He knew how to price the wines and the dishes. He was masterful in reducing obsolescence in the kitchen and upselling the most profitable items on the menu. His employees, customers, and partners could see, feel, and taste his competence.

Fast forward to a few years ago. On my way to the airport while facing a delayed flight, I stopped by his restaurant in Culver City, now the hub of innovation and a part of Silicon Beach with Google, Yahoo, and other technology giants nearby. He had purchased the entire shopping mall and was running three restaurants from that location. He told me that he had also opened another restaurant in Marina del Rey. He showed me the computerized systems he had in place to control the operations. He had automated systems that managed the people and advanced programs to build menu items and measure profitability. Roberto was a competent leader. And he did it consistently.

Assuming a leadership position does not necessarily require competency, but effective leadership always does.

Don't bet on the world being incompetent in order to become extraordinary. Weave the desire to be extraordinary into your PEP — develop a constant desire to become more competent. Look at your competence before you attempt to put your vision into effect. Then choose to take the responsibility of filling the gaps, not once, but always. That is the way you turn your competency into results.

"Courage is not the absence of fear,
but rather the assessment that something else
is more important than fear."
—Franklin D. Roosevelt,
32nd president of the United States

---<>---

To become a great leader, shape your original and unique PEP and let it guide your leadership talents. Become a transformational leader when you choose to lead. For years, a nobleman prayed each night to win the lottery. One night, he heard a voice from above exclaim, "You have to buy a lottery ticket first." To be a great leader, you have to first be YOU and fully realize your inherent leadership qualities within. Then, meticulously and constantly, identify the right situations to apply the variable dimensions of your talents. To be a good leader, you have to shape your very own style which is rooted in your PEP. A unique leadership style that is sensitive to the factors you cannot control – the uncompromising realities, the personal traits that you can tap into as channels of expression, and the actions and behaviors at your disposal through your axiom of choices.

The Legos of leadership principles – the axiom of your choices - are all always at your disposal. Not all pieces must fit well together before you start leading; never are all principals at play simultaneously. No one has achieved a one hundred percent perfect score and no one ever will. Because the scale of measurement and degree of applicability for these leadership principles are always in flux and situational.

---<>---

Next, let your leadership count for something tangible; let it turn vision to reality and drive you and your team to results.

Next, learn to travel past **THE LAST MILE**, not once but over and over as you choose, innovate, execute, change, and evolve.

CHAPTER SIXTEEN:

THE LAST MILE

In telecommunications, the "last mile problem" is getting the fiber-optic lines to your home or place of business: a necessary connection to secure service. In supply chain lexicon, it is effective delivery of goods from distribution centers to customers. In entrepreneurship, the last mile problem is what it takes to get ideas turned into crystallized value – into desired consequences.

To thrive, you must first begin. To stay in motion, you must first be in motion. Turn the energy of your wanderlust and your creativity into actions and outcomes. Execute and link your aspirations to results. Every time you endure the last mile and execute your way through it, you create a new version of yourself – you thrive.

"Knowing is not enough; we must apply.
Willing is not enough; we must do."
—Johann Wolfgang von Goethe, German writer and statesman

---<>---

When it comes to execution, hard work matters. It helps you refine yourself. It is more than a means to an accomplishment. It is a pathway to appreciation. When you travel far and work hard to get to the last mile, you appreciate the journey more. Hard work is important, but it does not solve the last mile problem. It is just not enough. Hard work may polish a man's soul, as a wise man once advised me. It may pave the path for the journey. But it is your intentions and beliefs that influence the intensity and the direction of your travels.

Gary Zukav, an American spiritual leader, argues that "Every action, thought, and feeling is motivated by an intention, and that intention is a cause that exists as one with an effect." Therefore, since your intentions are the cause of your actions, your intentions are also driving the effects – the consequences of your actions.

As you are responsible for the intentions behind your choices, you are also responsible for the consequences.

Intentions are rooted in the beliefs that influence your emotions and behaviors. The ABC cognitive behavioral model suggests that when you face Activating (A) events or triggers, you act based on the thoughts that occur to you: your Beliefs (B) at that moment. Your reactions are therefore Consequences (C) of your beliefs. In psychology, the triggering event is described as an interaction between you and people or situations; your belief is what your explanation is about why the triggering event has happened; and the consequences are the feelings and behaviors that your belief has caused.

In entrepreneurship, however, beliefs that only drive "feel good" outcomes are more often disruptive than productive. Your choices have more consequences than how you feel or behave. They define who you become. The consistency and clarity of your intentions and beliefs are critical to execution. They are paramount to solving the last mile problem. You will get lost in your journey when you apply your wanderlust to misguided intentions and confused beliefs. Let your PEP help you untangle situations with constancy across your journey and all triggering events.

Confusion is the enemy of execution.
Confusion in beliefs is the biggest foe.

Execution is not about force, mandates, or leadership. Exertion does not require you to be in the front of the pack with the widest view of the road; you don't have to be the lead dog. It is about realizing the important role of every other dog in the pack. Unleash the powers of everyone in your ecosystem (in your ocean) and exponentially increase your chances of success. To exert and execute is to create space for others to contribute, but it also closes the gaps that separate accomplishments. It is to make it safe for people to speak, to act, and to create. It is to care and make others care. It is to connect your power of thinking and doing with the power of others. It is to systematically complement your wanderlust to that of others; to expand the dimensions of your prosperity and accelerate your growth.

Your purposeful wanderlust provides the energy; your intentions and beliefs influence the intensity and direction. Hard work gets you focused to endure the journey. But pushing through the last mile requires more than vigor, exertion, good intentions, or consistent philosophies. It also requires more than your perceived strengths. You may see your abilities first, but should never let them define your role. Rob, an accomplished CEO and founder of a service and technology business, was a great salesman and visionary. But he often struggled in getting past the last mile, particularly as his ambitions were expanding beyond his plateaued revenue of about $10 million annually. His future success was compromised because his execution approach was centered around his strengths. When he realized that his true abilities could only rise from the depth of his inabilities and his transformational mindset, the game changed! Confusions were exposed, beliefs began to form and reform, and execution was focused. You, too, should apply the energy of your wanderlust to explore your shortcomings. You need not be an expert in every field in your organization, but you must not be ignorant of your weaknesses.

When it comes to execution, nothing is ever perfect. You will always face external barriers to demolish or navigate. There is always a laundry list of internal resistance factors such as time constraints, skill deficits, technology barriers, personal biases, and organizational habits. To overcome these barriers, don't start by being bound by the past, or by procedures and best practices. Entrepreneurial execution goes beyond following formulas to address standard problems. Get around the obstacles by being a *juggad* (in Hindi: जुगाड़): a non-conventional and frugal innovator. Look for solutions that do not obey conventions. Solutions hidden in the unknown. If you are bound by "how-tos" and best practices, your innovation is limited to that of others. Use "how-tos" to learn, but never make them the recipe for your life or entrepreneurship. Let the wisdom of different ages teach you. Learn **desire** from the millennials and **humility** from the golden generation. Learn **hope** from an eighty-year-old, **salesmanship** from a seven-year-old, **security** from a sixty-year-old, **ambition** from a teenager and **commitment** from a forty-year-old.

There is no one last and final last mile.
There are many.
Perhaps, as many
as the choices you make.

To go the last mile is the desire of every entrepreneur with an activated and purposeful wanderlust. To push past the resistance lines and to execute, swim the distance inward and flow past the unknown and the unforeseen, over and over. Always look for the last mile to travel. Look to get past the finish line in order to get to the results. Then, rush back to the starting line. Be always ready to face adversity as you construct your jagged path through the mountain of uncertainties. Energize your journey with your wanderlust. Let your wanderlust purposefully generate the sparks, let it trigger the flares that can clear your path forward. The fires that burn away your old obsolete behaviors and create new frontiers for growth.

Kindle and be on fire. You, your talents, your choices, your decisions, every one of your actions and your authentic soul are your firearms – your armament.

"The most powerful weapon on earth is the human soul on fire."
—Ferdinand Foch, French general and military theorist,
Supreme Allied Commander, WWI

---<>---

Next, get ready to travel **THE JAGGED PATH** of life and entrepreneurship. Let it keep you in motion. Let it drive you to be unreasonable and seek more change.

Learn to be your kind of innovative.

CHAPTER SEVENTEEN:

THE JAGGED PATH

Isaac Newton, the English mathematician, astronomer, theologian, author, and the father of modern physics, proved that a body at rest stays at rest, unless there is a force that compels it to move. He also showed that a body in motion stays in motion, unless other opposing forces impede its movement. Let your inherent need to explore, your wanderlust, be the force that compels you to move. Don't let the gravitational force of sameness hamper your continued movement. Stay in motion. Stay ready to push through the last mile over and over and travel through the jagged path of life and entrepreneurship.

A body in motion stays in motion, but in life and entrepreneurship, your motion is never on a straight line.

Your path is always jagged and never the same. Isaac Newton stated, "I can calculate the motions of heavenly bodies, but not the madness of men." At all times, the choices and consequences faced by men are infinite, uncertain, and not mathematically deterministic. They appear mad and irrational. Let your undefinable human madness, your desire to explore the unknown, and your unreasonableness in accepting sameness be the forces that keep you in motion.

"The reasonable man adapts himself to the world:
the unreasonable one persists
in trying to adapt the world to himself.
Therefore all progress depends on the unreasonable man."
—George Bernard Shaw,
Irish playwright and political activist

As an escaped slave who became a prominent activist, Frederick Douglass was reasonable in his cause but unreasonable in his approach. He realized that "It is not light that we need, but fire; it is not the gentle shower, but thunder. We need the storm, the whirlwind, and the earthquake." Like Douglass, be the wanderlust who challenges taboos. Be unreasonable in what you deserve, but very reasonable in how to get it. Be rational, but not constrained by claims of irrationality. Dare to challenge the normal perceptions and the habitual conclusions. Look for the abnormal and the unthinkable.

Be unreasonable, be an innovator.

---<>---

To be an innovator, explore ordinary situations and form unordinary perspectives. Genuine innovators, however, are not just searching for ideas, but for outcomes. They are not just in motion for the sake of being in motion. They are looking for the force, the outcome, that propels even more progress.

Innovation is the result of your guided and purposeful wanderlust. It is the bridge that connects your entrepreneurial talent and your abilities and capabilities to results.

**Innovation is not the end
that justifies the means,
but the means that are
required to get to the end: results.**

---<>---

Innovators are unique. Clayton Christensen, an American academic and business consultant, pursued research which suggested that "each individual innovator studied had a unique innovator's DNA for generating breakthrough business ideas." In other words, innovators are all different and enjoy different PEPs. His research revealed that "innovators rely on their courage to innovate – an active bias against the status quo and an unflinching willingness to take risks – to transform ideas into powerful impact." Christensen frames innovation from a lens of disruption that is triggered by the complacency of established companies. As they focus on defending their success, hungry newcomers (startups) begin to challenge for leadership. The rise of Netflix and the demise of Blockbuster in the home movie distribution industry is a vivid example of disruptive innovation. Fred Wilson, a venture capitalist and partner at Union Square Ventures, views business model innovation as the path to disruption. Find new creative ways to deliver products and exchange value with customers at a lower cost and you are innovative – like Salesforce and Facebook.

Ben Thompson, an American business, technology and media analyst, is the author of *Stratechery,* a subscription-based newsletter and podcast. Thompson claims that innovation comes from seamlessly integrated products that transform the customer experience; innovative products like the iPhone and the iPod and its predecessor, the Sony Walkman. Jeff Bezos, the founder of Amazon, views innovation from a customer experience perspective.

He believes that "customers are always beautifully and wonderfully dissatisfied, even when they report being happy and business is great." This perspective encompasses not only product but also the non-tangible experience. Bezos sees the constant dissatisfaction of customers as the never-ending source of innovation opportunities. Stewart Butterfield, a Canadian billionaire and the co-founder of the team-messaging application Slack, focuses on human behavior and suggests it is not the product or the experience that defines true innovation, but the ability to trigger a lasting change in customers' behavior. Examples of changed behavior are evident in the impact of Waze on how we navigate traffic, Twitter and how we communicate in short form, and Spotify on how we discover and listen to music.

The commonality in the unique perspective of different thought leaders towards innovation is the "creation of new value." Whether the path of discovering innovation opportunities is through exploring products, business models, human behavior, dissatisfaction, or disruptive opportunities, the objective is creation of new impactful value – outcomes. A desire that is often hidden within creative minds and handcuffed by confined intellect and externally imposed presumptions. Assumptions that ignore your inherent entrepreneurial talent and your innate ability to innovate.

"The creation of something new is not accomplished by the intellect but by the play instinct acting from inner necessity.
The creative mind plays with the objects it loves."
—Carl Jung, Swiss psychiatrist and psychoanalyst,
father of analytical psychology

---<>---

To be an innovator, fuel your innate drive (wanderlust) and make it purposeful. Push through the obstacles and opposing forces in order to stay in motion. Be an innovator, purposefully curious with galvanized wanderlust, an intense observer who asks questions with intent. Be an innovator, an active connector who explores ideas, situations, and people and looks for insightful links or disconnects. Be an innovator, an active learner, who can help bridge the intersection of ideas, activities, people, and experiences. Be an innovator, a seeker of constraints and frustrations, and find the elements that beg to be challenged and changed.

Research conducted in 2012 by the consulting firm McKinsey & Company, which included over 2,500 executives working at 300 companies, suggests that there are eight dimensions of behavior and focus that separates the innovation winners from others. The research suggests that the innovation journey begins with "aspiration" or the specific desire to want more. Next comes the courage to choose, the tenacity to discover, and the commitment to evolve the organization to embrace the new and remain ready to extend it over time. The last step is to mobilize by motivating, rewarding in order to innovate repeatedly.

> *"Innovation is the result, not the cause."*
> **—Pony Ma, CEO and chairman of Tencent**

---<>---

You learn to innovate by innovating. You learn to experience by experiencing. When you wander in circles, you compromise your masterpiece. Motion does not necessarily translate to innovation and tangible results. Imagine a six-inch by six-inch metal box, with two mechanical boxers with colorful shoes and shorts facing each other on the top. The figurine champions stand in form, motionless, waiting for a kid to turn the switch on. For as long as the toy has batteries, the puppet boxers beat each other up. The boxers dance, they demonstrate motion and eagerness to win, but there are no winners! The intensity of our efforts does not directly correlate to innovative outcomes. When we confuse efforts with results, we are merely figurine champions.

You learn to win by winning, not just by staying in motion.

Innovators seek to stay in motion regardless of the jagged path ahead. They apply their lust to wander to explore the unsolved, to destroy the gravitational force of sameness and the status quo and to discover new ideas and choices. Innovators stay in motion in order to exchange what they have with something of higher value – they dance!

---<>---

Next, get through the battlefields of execution, perform, and get to results. Learn to **BE A DANCER.**

CHAPTER EIGHTEEN:

BE A DANCER

"Opportunity dances with those already on the dance floor."
—H. Jackson Brown, Jr., American author

Dancers are authentic, as they creatively express the music and story line using their unique solo movements. They also stand ready to be choreographed and appreciate the value of a dance company, a team, as they know solo performances are few and far between. Dancers realize the value of effective communication and trust; every dancer knows how essential it is to respond to others' cues on the dance floor for the flawless execution of moves. Dancers navigate the risk of injury or a fall with every performance. They push through the pain of sprained ankles and permanent calluses. Dancers have the courage to face the music day after day.

In entrepreneurship, dance to remove barriers and find new footings. Shift your focus to stay relevant and conceive new competitive fronts while managing and maintaining. Dancers are shifters but are NOT shifty! They are neither evasive nor sneaky. Dancers are purposeful change agents with clarity of thought and timeliness of actions. They are in tune with the tempo of their surroundings and ride the rhythms. Great entrepreneurs are simultaneously both shifters and sustainers. They are dancers and movers who are confidently anchored in every step yet ready to pivot to the next move, able to alter their focus over and over while remaining true to their core, their unique PEPs.

To dance, you need to possess motivation and determination; you need to be able to focus and have the discipline to drive for perfection. To be a dancer is to be aware of the stage, the music, the surrounding obstacles, and your body's movements. To be a dancer is to have control over weight and balance in motion – to be able to shift and pivot as needed.

Enjoy a genuine love for dancing, the passion to express your uniqueness and creativity through choice and movement ... Be a dancer: an entrepreneur.

---<>---

Great dancers can execute moves in a perfectly choreographed manner or improvise by adjusting their movements to the state of their mind and body, the music, and the audience. In all cases, dancers stand ready to shift and pivot to the next move. Because, at its core, dance is about movement and change. So, too, is entrepreneurship.

Dancers shift to create harmony, to learn, to discover new choices, and to create; so do entrepreneurs.

Practicing entrepreneurs are great dancers. They dance to the rhythm of life and its opportunities. They dance with choices and consequences. They are motivated and dedicated. They have a sense of timing and are always ready for movement and execution. Entrepreneur dancers are aware of situations and obstacles that surround them, and stand ready to pivot and shift to balance capabilities and desires. They understand the value of choreography in plans and the need and challenges of solo performances. They are aware of their entrepreneurial talents and capabilities and remain unafraid of falls and failures. They dance to transform and shape their tomorrows and their ever-evolving unique sculptures.

Dancing fuels transformation, and dancers are transformers.

---<>---

DIMENSIONS AND MOVEMENTS

Dancers express their talents and messages in space, time, and form. Entrepreneurial dance also has three dimensions: Perspective, time, and shape. As an entrepreneurial dancer, you have the ability to change your perspective within the space you perform and compete, without losing focus. You can be a problem solver and a problem finder concurrently; **a perspective shifter**. You can operate in the present and in the future simultaneously without getting lost in the journey; you can be **a time shifter.** You can be a visionary who fuels innovation while remaining fully aware of the realities of execution. You can express with the right form and movement; you can be a **shape shifter.**

The Perspective Shifters

Perspective Shifters are the problem solvers that don't rely on others to define problems for them. They are finders and solvers rolled into one. By shifting their perspectives, they break the boundaries of both the problems and the solutions.

Every day, millions are being trained to be problem solvers: an army of close to 200 million college graduates worldwide, according to UNESCO. However, this problem-solving force is vulnerable! They may attack and decisively win the wrong battle as they address the wrong questions and solve the wrong problems. They are experts in solving the problems they are pointed to with the tools they have been handed and the thinking framework they have become familiar with. They are not, however, trained to find the *right* problems. When you shift your perspective, you position yourself to discover more. When you change your frame of reference, you let yourself learn more.

A fundamental part of every manager's role is finding ways to solve problems. Being a confident and skilled problem solver considerably increases your ability to be a successful manager. But it does not guarantee your success as an entrepreneur. You must be a problem solver, as well as an entrepreneurial dancer, a shifter who also identifies and anticipates problems. Change your perspective "on the fly" and become a problem finder. Be a gold miner and discover your next gift!

"Every problem is a gift. Without them we wouldn't grow."
—Tony Robbins, American author, coach,
motivational speaker, and philanthropist

Problem Solvers: From Methods to Connections

Research by Ann Graham Ehringer, a strategic consultant and coach to CEOs and senior executives, suggests, "Entrepreneurs' most significant, far-reaching, strategic decisions deal with conflict, dilemmas, and paradoxes that do not lend themselves to conventional approaches and structured decision making." Entrepreneurs claim that although they may use the general learning of past choices to solve these unorthodox problems, they are often unable to replicate situations; they need new paradigms and new principles for judgment. Ehringer's research also shows that most practicing entrepreneurs see themselves as "always in the middle," where the world around them is constantly being constructed, usually without a clear or predefined plan. As decisions are made and objectives met, the outcome and the process become the facet of another problem: a challenge or opportunity to innovate. Problems are always waiting to be found and competitive advantages are in hiding, waiting to be realized.

Be always in the middle. Be purposefully curious and look for new connections. View every issue, outcome, success, or failure as an opportunity, a connection point to the next decision. Shift from one connection point to the next in order to find the next advantage, innovation, and opportunity. Look through the lens of your Oceanness; examine your ecosystem and connections.

As a perspective shifter, you are a connection seeker and problem finder. In addition to tackling realized problems you explore connections, contemplate relevance, and seek solutions to problems that have not fully crystallized. Find them and allocate resources against your high probability hunches.

Solving requires targeted decisions; finding requires a probing mind! To realize your full entrepreneurial capabilities, you need both!

Problem Finders: From Connections to a Transformational Mindset

Being a perspective shifter begins with the correct mindset. A mindset that offers a desire to reframe problems. Thomas Wedell-Wedellsborg's research results, outlined in the *Harvard Business Review* article "Are You Solving the Right Problems?," suggested that over eighty-five percent of executives agreed or strongly agreed that their organizations were bad at problem diagnosis and an overwhelming majority agreed that the flaw carried significant costs. The research suggests that part of the problem is over-engineering the diagnostics process. The other part is "digging deeper into the problem they've already defined rather than arriving at another diagnosis... But creative solutions nearly always come from an alternative definition of the problem." In other words, people often look for a problem that existed before or can be addressed by best practices- problems that have "perceived clarity."

As a problem solver, you should be focused on solving a well-defined problem as opposed to finding or redefining the right problem.

Disney has mastered the art of redefining problems. Close to 150 million people visit Disney entertainment parks globally every year (pre-COVID-19, of course). All guests wait in lines to get on rides and enter exhibitions. Operations research experts (relabeled as data scientists) have wrestled with wait time and queuing challenges forever – optimizing capacity, demand, and all other delivery constraints that impact service levels. But Disney has redefined the problem and has looked beyond mechanical optimization approaches. Disney has identified the "long lines" as a psychological and a financial problem. The problem was not that lines were long, but that people were frustrated. The issue was that Disney was losing money while people waited in lines and couldn't purchase food and merchandise. To solve the redefined problem,

Disney created transparency (people get to know the wait time via mobile apps), focused on movement (made the lines move in a snake line format), offered attractions and food along the side of the line or nearby, introduced FastPass (a way to sign up for a ride, get a specific ride time, and then roam around the park and come back on time), and managed crowds on the fly (using wristbands and other technology to see the pattern of crowds and devise ways to balance ride capacity). By redefining the problem, Disney is addressing both the money and frustration problems, which are redefined problems that are at the core of the wait time optimization challenge.

> *"You can focus on things that are barriers*
> *or you can focus on ... redefining the problem."*
> **—Tim Cook, American business executive,**
> **philanthropist, engineer, and CEO of Apple, Inc.**

In his book, *How Not to Be Wrong*, Jordan Ellenberg offers a short and simple story that points to a life and death difference of redefining problems effectively.

During World War II, lots of Navy planes were downed by German antiaircraft fire. The solution appeared to be the installation of some sort of shielding layer on the plane, an armor covering the body and wings to protect against bullets. So, they examined the planes coming back from the battlefield and put extra armor in the areas that attracted the most fire. However, the hit and crash problem was not solved. They had found an obvious solution to the wrong problem! If the plane made it back to the base, it meant that the bullet holes and the damage they caused were not that serious or dangerous. The planes with serious damage crashed before ever making it back to safety for evaluation!

By redefining the problem, Abraham Wald, the Hungarian-born mathematician, suggested that what needed to be done was to armor up the areas that, on average, didn't have any bullet holes. Because aircrafts with bullet holes in those areas never made it back!

Wait before you solve! Find or redefine the RIGHT problem first.

Let your wanderlust, your purposeful curiosity, guide you towards discovery of new problems. Let it put you on the path to redefining the old. The curiosity which will drive you to ask, "Why?" And ask it again and again. To ask "What else?" To ask "How else?" Your ability to change your frame of reference, shift your perspective, and expand the number of lenses you see the situations through, will help you discover and learn more. Your humility and courage will empower you to explore your Oceanness and seek more knowledge from others. Your mindfulness and aviator qualities will guide you to accept uncertainty and navigate through probabilities and risk as you experiment your way to solutions. Let your entrepreneurial talent become the force behind the magic of your problem finding, redefining, and solving.

> *"Great problem solvers are made, not born...*
> *they are at their brightest best,*
> *when conditions of uncertainty are at peak."*
> **—Charles Conn and Robert McLean,**
> **co-authors of Bulletproof Problem Solving**

Be careful of thinking something is obvious. It is a great vulnerability. The second you fall into the "obvious" trap, you have taken your first step towards ignorance.

Never be fooled by the obvious. Never forget to change your frame of reference. Never approach a problem with the same perspective twice.

---<>---

There are three tempos practicing entrepreneurs dance to simultaneously. There are different kinds of problem-finding approaches and personalities, but three parallel discovery paths that great practicing entrepreneurs explore simultaneously and constantly!

If you are constantly on the hunt for improvements, you are an "Efficiency Hawk." You realize that every dollar saved is a dollar made. You understand that wasted time, efforts, and resources equal wasted profits. You look for problems in systems, procedures, and processes. Another group of problem finders are "Tree Shakers and Fruit Pickers." You wait for the low hanging fruits to reveal themselves, you discover the more obvious problems with more definable solutions and realize quick wins. The last, and most rare, group of problem finders are the "Destiny Spotters." You shape the organizations' destiny by continually looking beyond the bend in the road. You aim to find opportunities today that may become a problem for the market and competitors tomorrow. You look for problems before they are impactful or noticeable. You take responsibility for generating the evolutionary energies, triggering magnifying waves or even tsunamis that help companies evolve.

Problem-solving is simplified by using methods, systems, and predefined processes. Problem finding is more complicated and involved. It is more of a mindset triggered talent, a constant effort that begins with purposeful curiosity powered by true critical thinking. First, try reframing what is observed or experienced; find a problem that was previously defined in a certain way and define it differently in order to expand the solution sets. Second, aim to discover an entirely new problem.

To be a skilled perspective shifter, you need to be both a skilled problem solver and an expert problem finder. You need to be ready to constantly shift from one mode to the other. Never compromise one path of discovery for another. Let your creativity be ever at its best.

"Problems are nothing but wake-up calls for creativity."
—Gerhard Gschwandtner, Austrian author

The Time Shifters

Great problem finders are often "Time Shifters." Time Shifters are aware of the connections in their journey and always examine how tomorrow can be shaped given today's capabilities and yesterday's learning. They are constantly seeking "relevance" in the market and in products: relevance in the value they deliver to their customers, employees, partners, investors, and society. To stay relevant as a Time Shifter, you offer the right value at the right time. You realize that although one may become relevant and the timing may be right, unless the exchange formula (the relationship between what the customer pays versus the value proposition/service and product delivered) works, there is no real win.

All stand-up comedians know that with good timing a lame joke may get a laugh, but without it, the best material will fall flat. In business, good timing will bring you big laughs and continuous profits. Bill Gross, the founder of Idealab, believes that "timing is the single biggest reason that start-ups succeed." Amazon succeeded because the technology was mature enough to deliver the minimum viable service and people were starting to feel comfortable buying through a computer. Netflix, with its DVD subscription model, experienced initial adoption because Blockbuster had hooked customers on watching movies at home. Its follow up success in online delivery was well timed with streaming technology capabilities.

"Fling me across the fabric of time and the seas of space.
Make me nothing and from nothing - everything."
—Jalâluddîn Rumi, 13th century poet
and metaphysicist

The iPod was released in 2001, providing a platform for music lovers to buy and listen to what they liked, whenever they pleased. Roughly twenty years earlier, the Sony Walkman was born in 1979 and sold over 200 million devices which allowed listeners to take their cassette tape recorder everywhere and enjoy music at any time. Apple did not solve an unsolved problem or address an unserved need, but demonstrated excellent timing: capturing the opportunities presented by transitioning to a new platform, detaching music from physical means (tape or CD), and empowering users to buy online and on demand. Apple creatively redefined a solution to a problem previously solved! The Walkman was priced at $400 and iPod was introduced at closer to $550 (both adjusted for inflation); although expensive in both cases, the exchange (dollar for value relationship) worked well. Today, at under $10 a month, Spotify and Apple Music provide mobility and choice without the need for an additional initial equipment investment. Given the ubiquity of smartphones, the online music services have nailed "timing," "relevance," and "exchange" factors.

Dancers are fully aware that the magic of a great performance reveals itself second by second as movements reveal and interpret the music. In entrepreneurship, as in dancing, timing separates the star performers from the rest. As a time shifter you can transform yourself and your organization to become relevant, at the right time, offering the right value to your ecosystem of stakeholders.

The Shape Shifters

Finding the right problem and crafting the right solution is not enough. Being a visionary is not enough either. To win, you must be able to execute: navigate around production and sales challenges, make sure you have the working capital and the team to deliver, etc. You have to be able to transition – from finding a problem that creates a competitive advantage to connecting today's limitations to tomorrow's needs. You have to be able to manage and not just lead; manage by defining clear processes and activities and aiming for predictable outcomes. To lead transformationally, you need a clear vision and an appreciation of the realities of execution. You need to be trusted that results are achievable and trust your team in making the vision a reality

As an entrepreneur dancer, you have to execute every movement, manage every muscle (aspect of your organization), and embrace every note (market dynamics). In every performance, as a dancer, you have to seamlessly blend flexibility, timing, arranged moves, spontaneity, and creativity. You have to trust yourself and your company, and be ready for others to trust you. As a dancer, being academically acclaimed or technically superior does not necessarily guarantee a great performance. Every dancer knows that every stage has obstacles and every audience comes to the theater with different sentiments, emotions, experiences, and expectations. Practicing entrepreneurs are also aware of the constant presence of obstacles, the need for trust and the ever-changing nature of markets and customers. Every dancer, like every practicing entrepreneur, realizes that it is not the last performance that should define you, but the next one; that not all the pity and regrets can erase the past, but choices and actions can shape the future.

"The moving finger writes, and having written moves on.
Nor all thy piety nor all thy wit, can cancel half a line of it."
—Omar Khayyam, Persian mathematician,
astronomer, and poet

No two performances are alike. All dancers know that every performance is unique, done once and never repeated the same way. The same choreography may look different when executed by different bodies, capabilities, and attitudes. Regardless of the appearance of sameness, every dance is different and every dancer is unique. One dancer may be eloquent in slow moves and a master of balance while another brilliant at more athletically challenging sustained dance passages. Another dancer may enjoy a great deal of energy and speed but be unable to last long. Dancers articulate and project movement differently. Some move in a way that is tense, energetic, and even aggressive, others appear soft and fluid. Some phrase their movements - every detail is sharp and clear; others move in a way that one element flows into another. Some move exactly in time with the phrasing of the music; others express their movement somewhat independently of it.

No two lives or businesses are alike. No two entrepreneurs are precisely alike. As a practicing entrepreneur, as you dance with opportunities and choices, as you foxtrot, salsa, or rumba with the consequences of your choices, and as you rock, roll, turn, twist, pivot, and shift in time, perspective, and shape, you shape your next best version.

As a dancer, a practicing entrepreneur, and Shape Shifter, you must realize that you can never go back to the beginning, but you can make now the new beginning and change the ending. You must realize that there is always another performance ahead and stand ready to execute your moves flawlessly.

Shift your shape to see,
to explore, to understand,
to enhance and to create
your next advantages.
Shift it, over and over, in order to
shape and reshape the sculpture of YOU.

To shift is to go from managing activities and sustaining advantages, to acting as an inspirational leader who guides the organization to its next best version. As a Shape Shifter, you are simultaneously "**Number Crazed**," conscious of the dollars spent and the flow of cash through the organization, an "**Advantage Protector**," protecting the previously gained advantages and forcing change and innovation to maintain those advantages, a "**Capability Enhancer**," helping to boost your organization's competence on every front from technology, to people, capital, and access, and an "**Advantage Creator**," finding unsolved and significant problems as problem finders (Perspective Shifters), looking ahead and judging relevance, timing, and impact of those situations as Time Shifters, and balancing strategy and execution as Shape Shifters.

We are the fruit of our own decisions and the product of our own choices! We can choose sameness and view the world only through a static window, or be a dancer and shift our view over and over to gain more knowledge, make better decisions, and evolve. To create progress, learn to be Shape Shifters, Time Shifters, and Perspective Shifters, at will.

Learn to be a dancer. Because to be a dancer is to evolve, always.

---<>---

Being a dancer that moves to the tune of others is not enough.

Dancers are not just performance artists; their bodies are also the instruments through which art is created. As you learn to be a dancer, remember it is your life and your journey. It is your dance, **YOUR MUSIC, YOUR CHOICE.**

CHAPTER NINETEEN:
YOUR MUSIC, YOUR CHOICE

"Genius is the one who plays most like himself."
—Thelonious Monk, American jazz pianist
and composer

To make magical and moving music with a string instrument, shifting is essential. The position of the musician's hand on the vibrating strings tightly hugging the instrument's neck creates the music. Without their tender touch, there are no tunes. Without a shift, a movement of a finger from one position to another on the strings, no masterpiece can be created. You are an entrepreneur and all entrepreneurs are dancers and music makers. You get inspired by ideas, work hard to perfect your craft, and can collaborate with an orchestra - a team. Your timely shifts can lead to the creation of a successful outcome: pleasing music. But a misplay can ruin a great concert, a thriving business, or a promising project. To live and to evolve, to be an artist, a genius dancer, and to shape your sculpture, is to shift to the next position and to the next tune; it is to make music!

Shifters can feel the tempo of their organizations, the rhythms that shape the foundation or the culture of the company, the beat that drives innovation, productivity, communications, and more. As the company gets bigger, changing this tempo becomes harder, and the beats remain rather similar. The shift is occurring, the music is made, but there is a more predictable pattern to it. In organizations led by practicing entrepreneurs, changes happen faster, beats can vary quickly, and there is a greater focus on writing a better song than on creating a consistent experience.

Musicians, like dancers, are talented. Be a musician. Choose with one note, and one chord at a time, to make your unique music or elect to play a masterpiece created by another with your own twist, your unique shift and creativity. Like dancers, and entrepreneurs as they execute, every time musicians create a new piece or perform on stage, they demonstrate their authenticity; they navigate risk like a pilot. Successful musicians know their audience and build an ecosystem that fits who they are and helps them thrive.

Be a genius, a dancer and a composer with your every choice. You can make your music and choreograph your dance. You can color and shape your entrepreneurial talent. It is a choice; you can love your wisdom and form your PEP. How and when you shift drives the choices you make and the music you compose. How you ride that music defines your movements and your dance. One decision at a time, you chisel, form, and paint who you are; you outline the vastness of your Oceanness and give purpose to your wanderlust. As you shift, you fuel your imagination and your flight; you give life to your sculpture.

"Music gives a soul to the universe,
wings to the mind,
flight to the imagination,
and life to everything."
—Plato, ancient Greek philosopher

----<>---

To be the sculptor and the sculpture, to discover and pursue is not enough. To Ignite and discover is not enough, either. **NEXT**, you have to **EVOLVE AND BECOME.**

First, by **ACTUATING YOUR MINDFULNESS** and embracing uncertainty. Then, by learning the art of nervousness, the yin and yang of crisis, and more.

Stand ready and willing to align the stars in your favor. Make the choice: do not develop based on what has or will happen to you, but be what you choose to become.

"If the army of adversity rise to shed
the blood of the faithful,
I will join forces with the heavens
to root out its existence.
We will slash the dome of the heavens,
and create new reality."
—Hafez, Persian poet and philosopher

----<>---

<<END OF PART THREE>>

PART FOUR:
EVOLVE AND BECOME

*"Our inward power, when it obeys nature,
reacts to events by accommodating itself
to what it faces - to what is possible.
It needs no specific material.
It pursues its own aims
as circumstances allow;
it turns obstacles into fuel."*
**—Marcus Aurelius,
Roman emperor and Stoic philosopher**

*Because YOU Deserve MORE...
Because YOU can be MORE*

CHAPTER TWENTY:
ACTUATED MINDFULNESS

Be in the now, they say,
be mindful.
Be aware,
in control of your thoughts,
command your emotions
and your experiences.
Be free of judgment,
in the moment, they say.

Judge,
I say.
Be aware, but unsettled,
I say.
Be attentive
and not just appreciative.
Aware of connections, choices, and consequences;
attentive to changes, actions, and reactions.

Leave the contained
and the controlled.
Flow through time and
energize not just now,
but each and every moment to come,
I say.

Actuate your mindfulness and
activate your thoughts.
Unchain your experiences and
embrace your emotions.
Leave certainty,
and the illusion of control behind,
I say.

Escape from enlightenment in isolation
be more than the spark
found at the depth of meditation.
You are from gold,
be the fire, too.
I say.

Actuate your mindfulness,
I say.

Mindfulness is an inherent trait that can be cultivated. It is your basic human ability to be aware and attentive to what you are doing and when you are doing it. Mindfulness is not equal to being thoughtful and not the opposite of selfishness. You can be mindful only when you choose not to be oblivious.

"Zen teaches nothing;
it merely enables us to wake up and become aware.
It does not teach, it points."
—D.T. Suzuki, Japanese author

"Ordinary awareness" is being conscious of your emotional and intellectual reaction to experiences and situations. "Actuated mindfulness," on the other hand, is awareness with comprehension and insight that has a direct line to actions and results. It is much more than being nonjudgmental; more than pursuing complete awareness and control of your thoughts, emotions and experiences. It is about tangible progression, as well as regression. Mere awareness lacks connectivity to your Oceanness and the realization of your ability to navigate risk and shift your perception and future. Ordinary awareness does not lead to action; it ignores uncertainty and discounts judgment. Actuated mindfulness is an active state of mind and behavior. A vigorous state of learning and adjusting.

Inactivated and ordinary mindfulness is about the awareness of now through isolated introspection; actuated mindfulness is about turning that awareness into choices, decisions, and actions that shape every moment of your journey following the present minute. Where your wanderlust propels you to go and explore, your actuated mindfulness influences your choices and consequences and makes your wanderlust purposeful.

The mindful are aware that the past is the past and the future is always unsettled. When you practice actuated mindfulness, you bridge awareness to action, you turn sparks into fire. You connect the past to now in order to learn and explore the uncertainty of tomorrow and the possibilities for your next best version.

Actuated mindfulness is both the spark and the fire of change and growth.

Anguish is rooted in ignorance, delusions, misperceptions, and lack of clear comprehension. It is the disease that fills the vacuum in your life when mindfulness is absent. To improve your art as a sculptor, actuate your mindfulness. Constantly seek and gain knowledge about your reality that is always changing and becoming; be aware and attentive. Look to find "why" you strive and not "what" you strive for: the "why" that must be discovered, rediscovered, revealed, and refined with your every choice and action. Continuously gauge your "why" and improve your PEP. Listen, learn, compare, choose, act, and transform. There are always an infinite number of opportunities ahead, instances to choose and to evolve. You will realize your limitations when you get nervous and push the limits of your abilities. Look at every means as an end and every situation as a crisis that offers danger and opportunity. Your constantly changing life is influenced by the past, but it is not an extension of it. In every second and in every situation, you are facing a new world with connections, parameters, complexities, and choices that never existed before and that will never be available again.

Mindfulness is about directing energy.

When mindful, you are the fire that fuels the flames of sound judgment, constant preparedness, and effective execution. You are the spark that ignites creativity. You are authentic and enjoy the transformational awareness of a genuine leader. You are mindful when you navigate risk consciously and constantly; when you dance, pivot, and shift at the right time and for the right reasons. To be mindful is to be fully aware of your Oceanness and the reality that surrounds you. William Ward, the American poet, defines a pessimist as one who always complains about the wind, and the optimist as the sailor who leaves his future in the hands of destiny hoping that the winds will change direction. The realist, he suggests, adjusts the sails and is aware of the direction of the wind and controls the movement and journey. A realist is a mindful, practicing entrepreneur. Actuate your mindfulness and generate the continuous and transformational insights needed to evolve your PEP and the sculpture of yourself.

Be mindful. Acknowledge the power of one individual to envision and kick-start change. Realize the power of many to initiate, to reform, and to revolt. Stand ready to ignite or be ignited. Start the

YOU ARE NOT THEM
YOU ARE NOT THEM

fire in your belly. Let it grow, let it burn your biases, and clear a path to creativity. Let it help you become a better version of you.

--<>--

> *"The way we live history is not the way historians tell history.*
> *Our lives are messy and chaotic and bewildering."*
> **—David Grann, American journalist and author**
>
> Actuate your mindfulness, because the unforeseeable always awaits you and life is never perfectly in order, linear and predictable; life is messy.
>
> Next, explore and master the **PROMISING MESS WE LIVE IN**.

--<>--

CHAPTER TWENTY-ONE:

THE PROMISING MESS WE LIVE IN

*Accept the uncertainty of life
as the call for an adventure;
and it's messiness as
an opportunity for discovering
serenity, order and beauty.
An opportunity presented
every minute of every day,
to shape your future:
your next best version.*

Is life chaotic or orderly, deterministic or probabilistic? Do we deserve what we get? Do we get what we deserve? Is life truly a box of chocolates as claimed in the movie *Forrest Gump*? Can we pick what the future holds from a tray of sweet choices?

Some people believe that life is random. Others subscribe to destiny. Some claim life is a series of mutations that can be researched postmortem and justified scientifically. Others pronounce that life is a collection of independent choices directed by divine intervention.

Life often appears messy or, as the Chinese describe it, *Luan Qi Ba Zao*: a mess where all is in disorder. In fact, no one can be one hundred percent certain! The origin and future of the universe is still uncertain. Every minute of the day, millions of events are taking place, impacting the lives of billions of people. All actions and outcomes are subject to uncertainty! Life is not an IKEA bookcase that you can neatly assemble by following instructions. Life and entrepreneurship don't come with instructions.

The future
remains uncertain
and always probable,
but relatively controllable.
The past, however,
may be describable,
but remains uncontrollable.

You have some level of probabilistic control over today, but as it becomes yesterday and more explainable, you lose all dominance over it. You can only control your memory and the way you describe events. You can be optimistic or fatalistic. You can believe in existentialism or essentialism. Regardless, you cannot dispute your role as either the subject of the events or the driver of choices and consequences. Without a doubt, you are a character in this theater, your life; a messy world that is constantly changing and for the most part uncertain.

Entrepreneurs, by definition, seek to exchange one thing (a product service or situation) for another of higher value, knowing that the outcome of this exchange is uncertain. Our talent for entrepreneurship is explored only in uncertainty. When mindful, you are fully aware that life is messy and all exchanges are probabilistic. You are conscious that your choices have non-deterministic consequences. You realize that your decisions do not guarantee, but impact what you get in life. You acknowledge, with certainty, that your actions and reactions influence what you deserve and what you achieve in an uncertain world.

Early in my career, I was fooled by the notion and the allure of "certainty." I was trained to plan for alternative versions of the future, or MECE: Mutually Exclusive and Collectively Exhaustive scenarios of tomorrow. I assumed that in our connected world there was a real mutual exclusivity in business and life. I assumed that there was a chance in hell to explore all versions of the future and, despite its complexities, get to an exhaustive collection of possibilities. **I was wrong in believing that planning ensures certainty.**

--<>--

One evening at Boston Logan Airport, a very well-read but classically uneducated young man set me straight. Questioning my destiny and the value of planning and hard work, I met Sid (yes, he was named Sid, too!) at the airport bar while waiting for my plane back home. I was drinking away my sorrows after an unsuccessful series of meetings and events that were catastrophic to my business and hugely disruptive to my planned life at the time. Fortunately, Sid sensed my state of mind and initiated a conversation. I shared my thoughts and disappointment. "I am certain that we had all the bases covered," I declared. In response to my proclamation, he jumped into a discussion about Heisenberg, Plato, and the truth about an apple thrown up in the air.

Heisenberg's uncertainty principle claims that the position and the velocity of an object cannot both be measured exactly and at the same time. This principle exists because on a quantum level, a particle does not have absolute position and momentum simultaneously. Even if you try to control all observable and measurable factors in an experiment, you can never be assured of the results. That is to say, although with untrained eyes, we assume stability and are able to measure movement and position, in reality, there is no stability or certainty. Quantum mechanics explains that when all objects in the world are observed on a subatomic level, they are always in flux and never in an absolute and constant position and velocity.

*"If we know the present exactly, we can calculate the future;
it is not the conclusion that is wrong, but the premise."*
**—Werner Heisenberg, German theoretical physicist,
pioneer of quantum mechanics**

Building on the uncertainty principle, Sid argued that when you throw an apple in the air, you can never be certain of its exact path and turns. You apply a certain force which propels the apple up into the air while facing the resistance of gravity. The apple has a certain definable size and weight which impacts the visible speed and the height it travels. However, no two apples and situations are ever the same. The subatomic placement and movement vary and the exact number of turns of the apple, on its way up and back down to you, also vary. Heisenberg argued that since all is always in flux, every idea, situation, and experiment has a unique meaning. This applies to an apple thrown up in the air, just as it applies to every event in our lives and all of our entrepreneurial affairs.

Believe in the mystery
of 1,000 turns
# of an apple!

Over 2,500 years ago, Heraclitus of Ephesus (the ancient Greek philosopher) claimed that life is like a river. He observed that nature is in a state of constant flux: "Cold things grow hot, the hot cools, the wet dries, the parched moistens. Everything is constantly shifting, changing, and becoming something other to what it was before." Heraclitus claimed that we can't step into the same river twice because the river is constantly changing. The water flows, so when we step into a river the second time, we step into different water and thus a different river. Your entrepreneurial experiences and ecosystem are also subject to ebbs and flows; they are never the same. As a pilot navigating risk along your journey, every flight is always new. As a dancer, no two performances are exactly alike. As a leader, you never lead in the same situation twice.

Heisenberg scientifically proved what Heraclitus concluded by logic. You never face the exact same state and situation twice. You never step into the same river or the same life or business condition twice. Your decisions and their consequence (the apples you toss in the air) are subject to many ever-changing conditions (the turns of the apple).

There is no certainty in sameness, because there is no sameness. When all is in flux, all is uncertain.

Questioning the idea of an entirely uncertain universe, Einstein once said: "God does not play dice with the universe." I, too, had trouble accepting that we live in a one hundred percent uncertain world. A world where there is no certain predictability. A world in which all actions are connected and all reactions uncertain and probabilistic. A world where there is no solid footing, no stability, no anchors, and no real definable goal posts.

Airport Sid offered Plato's argument: all things are in flux, but we must distinguish between that which always is and never becomes and that which is always becoming and never is. Plato's

Theory of Forms asserts that all things in the domain of material are only shadows and images of intelligible concepts and forms. Where forms are unchanging concepts that transcend time and space, Plato suggests that "one should render himself immune to changes in the material world and strive to gain the knowledge of the eternal, immutable forms that reside in the intelligible realm."

The nature of the river and the number of turns of the apple are always in flux, but the fact that the river flows and an apple pitched in the air turns are always true. Your anchor is the core foundation of your beliefs, your life's philosophy, Sid suggested. The element that stabilizes your standing as you face flux and uncertainty. It is your inherent talents of comprehension, entrepreneurship, and leadership that immunizes you against change. It is your ability to decide, choose, and act. The more in tune you are with the intelligible forms, the more comfortable you are with uncertainty. The more mindful you are of your choices and consequences, the closer you are to your authentic self. The more you know, the more risk you navigate, and the less unwarranted risk you take. The degree of risk you face is inversely proportional to your embraced knowledge of situations. The more intense your love of your wisdom, the more certain you can be, in decisions and actions, while facing uncertainty.

On the plane ride back home, I decided that my power to shape the future is not rooted in my ability to plan for uncertainty, but to acknowledge that it exists. To embrace it. My focus should be on applying my talents to learning from uncertainty itself. To learn that, every day, life circumstances and alternatives are analogous to an apple thrown up in the air. To acknowledge that beginnings, endings, and situations are subject to 1,000 turns, new experiences never seen before. I realized then that life and outcomes are not subject to exhaustiveness or mutual exclusivity of my plans, but a function of my inclusivity of uncertainty in all of my thoughts: a function of my actuated mindfulness.

--<>--

Life and entrepreneurship are messy and ambiguous, but always pregnant with opportunities.

Imagine a line between any two points (A = beginning and B = ending). There are countless points, infinite, between the beginning (A) and the ending (B). Now imagine point "C" or a point anywhere between "A" and "B." The line between "A" and "C" also represents infinite points, so does the line between "C" and "B." Now consider "A" as the beginning of your life and B as the ending. Point "C" could represent you at any age, at eight or eighty. At any point and any age, there are an equal number of points (infinite) in front of you as there were behind you. Consider them instances (seconds and sub-seconds) at which you can make a decision. Each point represents an opportunity to make a choice. At any point in your life, there are endless opportunities for decisions and changes. Each decision brings about a series of consequences. Your choices are never the same because you are never at the exact same place; you are never stepping into the same river. The world is changing around you and your experiences are constantly changing you. When mindful, you realize that life is messy and probabilistic; you are also conscious of the fact that you always have choices awaiting your decision.

"Every second is of infinite value."

**—Johann Wolfgang von Goethe,
German writer and statesman**

Today, I realize today that whatever comes to me is from me, from my choices, and their consequences. Outcomes that are rooted in my decisions; choices made out of arrogance and ego colored with the assumptions of certainty; resolutions that are based on my ignorance of the power and influence of uncertainty.

One day, an eagle took off from a stone, looking
for prey, extending her wings.
She gazed at her stretched wings and proclaimed:
Today the entire world is under my wings
as I fly at the top of the skies, with my
magnificent eyes I will see the smallest objects
at the bottom of the seas
If a mosquito moves in a meadow,
his movement is crystal clear, with my amazing vision.

The eagle, as described by Nasser Khosrow, the Persian poet, was proud of her ability to fly high and her dominance of the skies. She was dazzled by the incredible power of her eyesight.

She was audacious and tainted with arrogance,
uncaring of destiny, life, and change.

Suddenly, from the hidden bunkers, an arrow was released.
It cut the skies, and landed in the eagle's side.
She descended from the clouds into the sludge of the valley.
Like a fish out of water struggling on the ground.
She wondered,
how could an arrow made out of iron and lumber
be so powerful and fast like thunder?

Astonished, the eagle was struck by an arrow and fell from the skies.

When she looked closer at her wings
she noted her own feathers were
guiding the arrow, giving it lift!

She whispered who can I blame?
It is from us that all comes to us.

The eagle realized that it is the power of her own feathers, designed to fly high, that have given the arrow its might.

I sometimes doubt that there was another Sid in Boston that day. But I don't hesitate to embrace his perspective. I aim to practice actuated mindfulness and strive to thrust past the limits of my thinking and doing. I stand mindful of my fears and force myself through them. I accept that every apple pitched in the air takes 1,000 turns and offers infinite opportunities. **I suggest you do the same because it is from us that all comes to us.**

----<>----

> If there are choices and decisions and probabilities, then there are failures and disappointments. It is indeed from us that all comes to us, including how we face failure.
>
> Next, let's explore how to find your path to wisdom through **THE WOUNDS OF FAILURE**.

---<>---

CHAPTER TWENTY-TWO:

THE WOUNDS OF FAILURE

The wounds of failure are the pathways to wisdom.

Failure is the bridge between the unknown and the known. When perceived normal, you fear, you fail, and you regret. When abnormal, you fear, you fail, and you *celebrate*. Practicing entrepreneurs are abnormal. If you are afraid of failure, it is normal. If you are afraid of learning from it and shaping a new you, it is unfortunate. All practicing entrepreneurs fear failure, too, but they are thirsty for knowledge, the love of the wisdom that enhances their PEP.

You can be afraid of failure, but you can also fear success. Before Margaret Thatcher became the prime minister of the United Kingdom, she made a key observation about America: "They are unafraid of success. We in Great Britain and in Europe are formed mostly by our history. They, on the other hand, are formed by their philosophy. Not by what has been, but by what can be. Don't be defined by your history and afraid of success. Learn, change, and evolve. However, just as you have to push through failure to grow, you have to push through success to gain clarity and untangle from history. Learning is the spark that starts the flame of the torch that brightens your path to the future; the forceful, purifying, and cleansing flame that clears your path to your next best version.

"You make mistakes. Mistakes don't make you."
—Maxwell Maltz, American cosmetic surgeon and author

Regret the mistake without learning and you have let the mistake make you. Learn and you have gained experience and automatically succeeded. To be unaware that failure awaits you is to embrace a shallow success. That is when you truly fail; when your failure makes your regrets justified. Fail to learn from your failure and you have made a mistake.

In an attempt to acknowledge the tremendous value of time to get to results, some promote "failing fast and often." Regardless of speed and frequency, you only fail when you don't learn. Aspire to learn fast from your actions and that of others, but never *intend* to fail. Failure is not success; it must not be a goal. Don't aim to fail but don't waste a failure, either.

Avoid the tragedy of wasted failures, Always be ready to shift from failing to learning.

---<>---

Most race car drivers prefer a manual transmission to an automatic one. They like the power that stick shift vehicles provide them. It gives them the ability to control the acceleration at sharp turns and the speed to overcome a competitor on the racetrack. The ability to shift empowers them to navigate around the risk of collision and position themselves to win. In today's business race, entrepreneurs need to stand ready to make quick and potentially transformational decisions in the face of changing customer expectations and innovative competitors.

Often, leading a large organization (the domain of contained entrepreneurs) is more like driving an automatic car, where the machine's reliability, consistency in process, and the predictability of outcomes are considered a victory by market analysts. The corporate race is generally longer and much better financed. It is like the Daytona 500. To complete the race within three and a half hours, the driver has to do 200+ laps around the track or 500+ miles at an average speed approaching 150 miles per hour. To win, the driver has to stay in the race by avoiding collisions and, most importantly, avoiding mistakes. NASCAR on NBC analyst Steve Letarte suggests, "...not all mistakes are a mistake, sometimes you zig, and you just know the guy behind you is going to zig, and he zags. And you're done." In a large corporate setting, if you zig and the rest of the organization zags, you are set up for a definite collision. By comparison, in smaller, less structured, and more entrepreneurial settings, you are expected to zig and zag constantly as you maneuver through obstacles. Fail and learn. That is how you turn a potential mistake into an advantage.

Pilots know that when there is a flight, there is risk of failure. Risk that must be navigated around or accepted with knowledge of potential consequences. Dancers pivot their way to success. They shift from failure to learning. They shift to a new gear at the right time whether to slow down or speed up – always to gain more control.

Street race drivers are most like practicing entrepreneurs. They can begin anywhere, at a traffic light or while cruising next to each other. The real end point of the race is often unclear; there's no formal threshold to cross to win the race. Drivers are focused on getting and staying ahead quickly. Timing is everything and a fraction of a second late to start or missing a single shift can cost the driver a victory. At its most potent form, entrepreneurship, like street racing, is a fast and dangerous sport. Practicing entrepreneurs are able to organize, pivot, and shift swiftly to overcome competitors and "stay relevant." They stay aware of market timing and the turns in customer expectations. They are dancers, aware of the rhythm of the music and the obstacles they face. They shift constantly to position themselves for the right next move; they position themselves to succeed.

> *"The secret of life, though, is to fall seven times*
> *and to get up eight times."*
> **—Paulo Coelho, The Alchemist**

Although the driver most often gets the recognition and glory, without the crew, wins are not likely.

Organized racing, like hockey, is a team sport and so is entrepreneurship. In ice hockey, a "line" is a group of athletes that play and compete as a group. The game is structured around four lines that shift in and out of the game – substitutions can occur even in the middle of a play. The line-mates courageously play against their strategy for the match. They define and redefine their roles, constantly. They are shifters. They shift on the fly – take an offensive stance, a defensive posture, or bring in the fourth line, the group of players often trusted to bring energy back to the game. Players are fully aware of the value of their ocean (their ecosystem) and the impact of their Oceanness on the game. They strive to connect, to be a provider, and to energize constantly.

In large corporate settings, positions are well-defined and interchangeability is limited. The primary aim is to increase productivity, which is frequently correlated to more streamlined processes. It is rare for corporate players to change positions rapidly and repeatedly, a key factor that limits contained entrepreneurs from unleashing their inherent capabilities. In early stage and more developed entrepreneurial environments, the ability to pivot is an important part of the game. The team members are always ready to shift, change their position, and join the game. It is the entrepreneur's Oceanness that generally facilitates the environment for this shift and lays the groundwork for a culture of togetherness and connectivity.

To reduce the risk of failure, change at will or orchestrate change swiftly; move from one state or condition to another and be willing to stick your neck out!

The only way to move forward is to stick your neck out, whether you are a rabbit or a turtle!

In a game, change the players at the wrong time (shift) and your opponent scores; in a race, speed up too fast as you approach a bend in the road and you are risking an accident. Good practicing entrepreneurs realize to learn fast and recover quickly they must dance and pivot again and again with purpose. The players are always playing to win, never to fail! However, they anticipate failures and are ready to turn them into knowledge advantages.

Jack Ma grew up in communist China. He failed twice at the national entrance exam before being accepted to university and was rejected from a dozen jobs before he founded Alibaba, the Chinese answer to Amazon and eBay. "If you cannot get used to failure — just like a boxer — if you can't get used to [being] hit, how can you win?" Ma emphasizes.

In bigger corporate settings, where failure is toxic, shifting comes with personal liability, another factor limiting contained entrepreneurs and executives and making them more cautious and likely to sway towards being a sustainer. George Lucas negotiated a $20,000 pay cut with 20th Century Fox in exchange for all of the merchandising rights to Star Wars, and all of the sequels thereafter. The nine blockbuster sequel franchise and merchandise sales have earned billions, making Lucas worth a reported $5.2 billion. According to Tom Pollak, Lucas's attorney at the time, the deal was made after Universal Studios passed on making the film and Fox had agreed to a total of $150,000 payment for Lucas's fees. Alan Ladd Jr. and Bill Immerman, studio executives who were involved with the transaction, continue to blame each other – Immerman says Ladd approved the deal and Ladd says Immerman did it on his own. George Lucas was able to look around the bend, live in the future, and negotiate his shift to fame and fortune. In parallel, the very capable executives (contained entrepreneurs) avoided corporate and personal exposure – or so they thought!

Broad institutionalized assumptions and perceptions based on biases can also drive mistakes. In search of their first record contract, the Beatles auditioned at Decca Records in London. The executive in charge of talent claimed that four-piece groups with guitars would not succeed. The studio thought they avoided a failure by sticking to common perceptions. Boy, were they wrong!

Well-planned initiatives can also lead to failure. Famously, in the mid-80s, The Coca-Cola Company aimed to do a product shift and introduced "New Coke," one of the best-known product introduction flops in American history. Sales dropped by twenty percent and the company responded by reintroducing the original product as "Coca-Cola Classic." If looked at as learning experiments that offer knowledge, failures are just "life moving us in a different direction," or at times tilting us back onto our original path. The Coca-Cola Company was able to face failure and had the courage to change course and get back on the path to success. Coca-Cola's actions turned a failed experiment into an advantage. Experimentation without failure does not exist and progress with "zero" disappointments is only a dream. Almost any time you shift to a new plan, you experiment and risk failure; you also create a path for learning. Fail to shift, experiment, and learn and you risk being stagnant and losing relevance. Fail to learn from a failure and a mistake is made.

To win you have to dance, to pivot and to shift, sometimes to avoid a hit and sometimes because of one!

As you evolve, success is never final and failure is rarely mortal. The will and the courage to exchange, to color your entrepreneurial talents, and to evolve is what counts; the courage to shape your next sculpture without the fear of breaking who you are. To have the courage to continue is to have the willingness to dance and pivot your way to a new winning position and risk failing again.

Have the courage to shift over and over, and the courage to acknowledge and stay away from the vortex of demise. You can shift to failures that are harmful and without any real knowledge benefits; behaviors that are directly in contrast to experimentation-driven and purposeful activities. Uncontrolled, unplanned, and unrestrained shifting increases the risk of failure versus mistake. It creates an inescapable vortex of demise. Pilots never shift to a new flight plan in midair without cause. Be erratic and you may risk losing your core beliefs and strengths. Mystical stories suggest that the more a Shape Shifter reconstructs into a new silhouette, the more they lose sight of their original form. When you shift to be reactive and in conflict with the tenets of your PEP, you are imposing unwarranted risk, creating strategic confusion, and triggering execution blunders. You are positioning yourself for failure.

After its blunder of opening multiple accounts for customers without their knowledge, Wells Fargo is becoming an excellent example of what not to do. On a call with the private banking group at Wells Fargo, a senior banker and his experienced team admitted that clients are not thrilled with them and that the bank is losing more clients than they are gaining. It is the response of the leadership to this "problem" that offers the learning experience: reorganize to have a multitiered private banking group with relationships that range from under a million to about $2 million, then $2 to $5 million and above (the ranges could be slightly different, so don't quote me!). When I questioned the team about how this reorganization would solve the problem of "lost trust," no one could defend it or even explain it. That is shifting deviously to solve the wrong problem.

Great entrepreneurs, like great dancers, have great control. They roll, they spin, and they turn. They shift to gain control and to be responsive. They do not exhibit erratic behaviors or deceptive moves that will lead them to imbalance.

Next, get ready to be nervous.

The probabilities and uncertain life that we live in promises crisis and both danger and opportunity. Life and entrepreneurship hold the potential for failure with every choice we face and trigger. Failures with wounds that are pathways to wisdom. When you push through your comfort zone and the limits of your sameness in order to evolve, you will risk failure and often face nervousness.

Next, acquire **THE ART OF BEING NERVOUS**.

CHAPTER TWENTY-THREE:

THE ART OF BEING NERVOUS

All big fires start with a single spark. If you're not nervous, you are not looking for a flame. You are not acting as the spark and you are not taking advantage of the energy nervousness creates. Most important, you are not mindful of the situation you're in.

All great artists, the masters of their domains, value nervousness. Tiger Woods, the professional golfer, believes, "If you're not nervous, it means you don't care." Miles Davis, jazz trumpeter, bandleader, and composer, suggests, "If you're not nervous then you're not paying attention." Michael Jordan, former professional basketball player, recommends, "Being nervous isn't bad. It just means something important is happening." Beyoncé, singer, songwriter, and actress, claims, "I get nervous when I don't get nervous. If I'm nervous, I know I'm going to have a good show." There is an art in being nervous. Great masterpieces and performances are all on the other side of your comfort zone. They are created because you cared, paid attention, and realized that what you do is important. All great artists push their limits and are nervous first! All winners start by being nervous, too. You are the sculptor; be nervous, be an artist who is perpetually creating. What matters is your next move!

"When making a painting, only one thing counts:
what you do next."
—Walter Darby Bannard, American painter

---<>---

If you are not nervous, either the challenge is not worthy or you are playing beneath your potential. Play the game of entrepreneurship at or above your potential, not at the limits of your fear. When you choose to make nervousness equal to fearfulness you make its energy destructive. Fear deteriorates your confidence and drives indecisiveness. The mindful strive to be nervous, but not fearful. Let your nervousness be the antidote to fear.

Every triumph begins with a desire to discover and to do – a lust to wander. Every victory requires awareness, a little nervousness, and the courage to overcome fears. Every success is shaped by mindfulness of choices, decisions, actions, and reactions. Learn to activate your mindfulness. When mindful, you can listen to and accept the thoughts and feelings that arise within you, the feelings of nervousness and excitement. When you are excited, you are focused on celebrating. When nervous, you are concentrating on learning, adjusting, and improving. First, be excited to be nervous. You have found something important to do and discovered a personal limit and barrier to break. Second, be mindful of your nervousness and turn its energy into a force. A force of movement and achievement. A force of triumph.

Anything worth doing, is something worth being nervous about.

You are nervous on the first day of school and every time you take a test. You are nervous as a soccer player or piano player at a game or a performance. You are nervous when you start a new job and nervous when you are laid off. You are nervous because your previously stable and seemingly certain situation is changing into an unknown circumstance. You are nervous because you are *aware* that you are facing a condition of uncertainty - a key element of mindfulness. When you direct the energy of the experience and your nervousness, you are *attentive* – another key element of mindfulness. You are mindfully nervous when you are both aware and attentive.

Practice the art of being nervous. Choose to be a little nervous because you deserve more. That is how you improve your sculpture, your masterpiece. Choose to use the energy of nervousness to stimulate your entrepreneurial talent. Apply the energy to exchange one resource (product, service, or situation) into another of higher value. Be nervous about being a pilot and navigating risk. Be nervous, because your journey is taking you to new places; because you realize your flight "checklist" may not be complete. Only then will you discover new risk factors. Be nervous when you shape and reshape your Oceanness, explore how to be a provider to your connections, and how to generate new waves that will influence the growth of your organization. Be nervous when you shift your perspective in order to gain new insight. Be nervous and always push yourself to learn your limits of authenticity. Be nervous as new situations call for your leadership. When you are mindfully nervous, you generate the energy that carries you to the edges of your abilities. It is at the edges that you discover, you learn, and you create. It is at your limits that you set your soul on fire.

Your anxiety about change and your fear of the unknown and uncertainty chain you to the past and sameness. You get nervous when you rattle this invisible chain. Actuate your mindfulness, look back and see the chain that is hindering your progress and impeding your movement. Then, break the chain and evolve.

---<>---

Failures and nervousness are reactions and outcomes, feelings and mindsets triggered by dangers and opportunities. Conditions that appear when we face situations that are not harmonized; situations that appear to be a crisis.

Next, explore **THE YIN AND THE YANG OF CRISIS** and harmonize the path of change – the always under construction road to your next best version.

CHAPTER TWENTY-FOUR:

THE YIN AND THE YANG OF CRISIS (危 机)

The mindful never waste a crisis because opportunities are hidden in chaos.

"Never waste the opportunity offered by a good crisis."
—Niccolò Machiavelli, Italian diplomat, philosopher, and writer

"Yin and yang" is a thousand years' old relational idea. It proposes that the universe is governed by duality and ruled by a set of two opposing and complementary principles or energies: the yin and the yang. One is negative and dark (yin) and the other positive and bright (yang). The principle of duality exists in all aspects of our lives and is hidden in all of our choices. The interaction of these contrasting, but harmonizing principles influences the future. It impacts your sculpture of self that you, the sculptor, shapes and reshape. The Chinese word for crisis is written with two symbols: danger and opportunity. This suggests that every crisis has both positive and negative components and offers the yin and the yang. This is the duality that can improve your personal philosophy and sharpen your chisel as you create your evolving masterpiece.

In a crisis, rely on your actuated mindfulness. Remain aware of the dangers and plan to contain them. Also be steadfast to explore the opportunities. Embrace a crisis when it presents itself. Play offense and defense simultaneously. Any crisis changes the balance between risk and outcome. If the outcome of a situation is less desirable than the status quo, then you must take more risk to achieve a better outcome. Like a pilot, start your risk navigation before the crisis is visible. Connect what is and what could be and build a bridge between failure and accomplishment. To be mindful is not just about predicting or preventing a crisis. It is about being prepared to make the crisis a passage to a new and competitive advantage.

A crisis is not a problem to be solved, but a situation you go through. Your aim is to harmonize the confusion.

---<>---

According to Oxford Dictionary, crises reflect "times when difficult or important decisions must be made." Hurricanes, economic meltdowns, and an invisible killer virus are impactful events. These are situations that require important decisions and reflect a crisis. A key employee quitting, a seemingly smart marketing campaign which backfires, the water pipes bursting in the warehouse, and a major supplier raising prices are also events that require major decisions. Launching a new product or service, implementing new technology, or revamping the sales model are also crises that require important and difficult decisions. A new baby, a divorce, and a death in the family are personal crises that impact your life and business. Crises come in all shapes and forms. Some are imposed upon you and have to be embraced. Others are self-inflicted by strategy or ignorance. Some crises turn deadly as bad decisions follow. Others lead to glorious competitive advantages. The SARS pandemic of the early 2000s helped catalyze the growth of Alibaba, the giant Asian e-commerce company. As people had to quarantine at home, the internet became essential and Jack Ma's team were ready to operate from home for long hours and utilize the infrastructure they had built for growth. Does this remind you of another crisis? Post 2008, Airbnb and Uber began to rise. Over fifty percent of Fortune

500 companies have their roots in a recession, including Microsoft, IBM, Hyatt, Google, Salesforce, and FedEx.

Some crises can be traced back to poor decisions, both before and after major events. Toyota developed a massive crisis in 2009. Due to unintended acceleration issues, the automaker recalled 7.5 million vehicles and had to suspend the sale of eight different models; a crisis that at one point was costing the company over $54 million a day. The company first claimed "no defect exists." Later, Toyota had to defend itself in front of the world and the U.S. Congress. In 2010, British Petroleum (BP) faced a crisis when a drilling rig in the Gulf of Mexico failed, causing one of the worst oil spills in history. It was a long and very public affair that cost the company tens of billions of dollars. Two tragic plane crashes of the Boeing 737 Max caused by the autopilot system during takeoff placed Boeing in a considerable crisis situation. A drive for early profits, rapid product release, and sloppy quality assurance were key instigators. When exposed, all these crises were labeled as Public Relations (PR) issues, causing the companies' financial decline and customer trust erosion. However, the bad decisions that followed the events only exaggerated the dangers. The unrealized threat was rooted in communication problems, leadership failures, lack of courage to change, and failure to realize uncertainties that contributed or caused the crisis that ensued. Don't try to avoid admitting mistakes and admit them early, without making excuses or claims that are likely to have to be retracted later. In that way, you can minimize the bad PR and maintain or at least regain customer trust.

Some turning point events, in people's and corporate lives, are rooted in mischief and malice. Equifax, the consumer credit rating company, faced a massive crisis when hackers stole private information from an estimated 143 million people. This crisis changed the viability of the company forever. The U.S. college admissions scandal that centered around wealthy parents bribing school officials to get their children into elite universities created a crisis for the top schools in the country. These crises are rooted in greed, a hunger for money and power on all fronts. Equifax could have invested in its cybersecurity infrastructure as opposed to focusing on more profits. Did Equifax become the victim of a crisis or did they bring it upon themselves? The lives of the students and the parents who paid to get into exclusive schools have changed forever. Could they have avoided the scandal and escaped the crisis?

When a car company introduces a new model but limits its production, it may be fabricating a crisis in order to create pent-up demand. When the Saudis, in a feud with the Russians, suddenly increased oil production and dropped prices, they created a global crisis in order to achieve market advantage. When the U.S. government assassinated an unruly Iranian general, Qasem Soleimani, in Iraq and risked war, it created a crisis. These are all events that involved change and important decisions initiated with a purpose and the knowledge of risk.

Big crises, always, hold the potential of becoming catastrophic. The pre- and post-crisis compounding effect of bad decisions often leads to worse outcomes. COVID-19 affected tens of millions globally and killed over a million...so far. Faced with massive global economic challenges, countries and leaders are looking for someone to blame. Someone, "not us", has to pay. Maybe the Chinese did not control the spread early. Maybe they did not reveal the approaching disaster in time. But their misbehaviors do not address the unpreparedness of the world. Bad decisions at one point and by one party do not reduce the impact and the responsibility of bad decisions at another point and by others! While some countries blame China, others are blaming the World Health Organization (WHO). The entire European Union (EU) coalition is facing scrutiny. The Italians and the Spanish are questioning Germany for failing to help them. The Americans struggled to get organized and the cracks of their internal political rivalries appeared as wide as a scary canyon and placed the country at risk. Regardless of cause, the role of poor decisions cannot be discounted. Years before the COVID-19 virus, a number of legislative bills were presented to the U.S. Congress asking for funding to prepare for such an event. None were funded because the threat was not deemed imminent. The leaders did not properly navigate the risk although it was disclosed. Economic devastation and blame can lead to wars, widespread economic depression, and famine. In crisis, and in life, every decision matters.

Crises are the outcomes, the consequences of choices.

Crisis represents a deviation from the norm and requires important decisions. In life and in business, abnormalities are normal. Crisis exposes the uncertainty that is hidden at the center of everyday life and business decisions. It reveals and communicates uncertainty. It signals that an old condition is perishing and a new one has not fully settled and become the new normal. Every ending is only a new beginning, and every beginning is an ending; both conditions represent crisis – deviations from the norm and situations that connect the past to the future. A crisis marks the beginning of a change and offers an opportunity to choose, sometimes immediately visible, like a burning flame, and other times concealed and instigating corrosion, rusting slowly.

There is a difference between burning and rusting. Both reactions are exothermic (they "produce" heat energy). Rusting occurs slowly and its thermal energy dissipates before there is a noticeable temperature rise. Rusting arises from sameness and staleness. Combustion, on the other hand, releases energy much faster causing a noticeable temperature increase, a bright light, and a flame. Rusting begins without the help of any external energy and leads to the slow demise of its victim, making the hardest metals coarse, flaky, and fragile. A heat source is needed for a combustive reaction that begins quickly and produces massive energy. In entrepreneurship, the mindful actively direct the energy, aim to control the fire's destructive aspects, and look to initiate progress and differentiation; they ignite competitiveness. The COVID-19 crisis represents a combustion: fast, destructive, and massive. The virus shined a spotlight on a system (U.S. healthcare) which was rusting and becoming more fragile year after year. General Electric (GE), the darling of Wall Street in the 80s and 90s, started its demise after the 2008 financial meltdown. That deterioration may have surfaced after the great recession, but its corrosion started years before with ignorance of the risks related to GE capital.

All systems eventually rust. And initiate a crisis. Often, it is better to ignite the combustion yourself and burn rather than to slowly rust away by looking the other way or choosing the comfort of no change. The frog enjoying a bath in a slowly warming pot may not realize the approaching crisis, but it is coming! The mindful will not wait for the water to reach a boiling temperature!

---<>---

Whether self-inflicted or imposed upon us, every crisis involves three defining stages: the moments of truth, the moments of anticipation, and the moments of imagination. When you consider the uncertainty of outcomes, you imagine alternative paths and actions; you become aware of the dangers and the opportunities. When you actuate your mindfulness, you act and become attentive. You anticipate outcomes rooted in your awareness and your choices. When your actions face consequences, you realize the truth. This is the moment your value proposition meets the customer or your decisions bear fruit. But it also is the moment to reimagine, anticipate the next choices and consequences, and act again: an opportunity to consider another crisis, an opportunity to evolve, again.

Be mindful. Let a crisis ignite your genius within. Your choices and decisions are compromised when your imagination is out of focus. Appreciate the value of imagination and anticipation and be purposefully nervous about the moments of truth. Always remember that crises are born pregnant with twins named danger and opportunity. Choose to be nervous about the crisis that is always around the corner. Consider initiating your own crisis in order to conceive a new reality. Never leave change to chance and don't waste a good crisis, a flame you can start or a fire you can take advantage of. Stand ready to gain wisdom from the wounds of your failures; the uncertainty of life and the dangers hidden in crisis hold the potential for disappointments.

A crisis reflects a path to change, a gateway to the next stage that runs through abnormality. You can only manage the side effects of a crisis, but not the crisis itself. Just as you can only manage the impacts of change and not change itself. Your mission is to harmonize the dangers and opportunities. Both crisis and change have to be competently embraced before their consequences can be managed. Stay competent and aware of dangers and opportunities, always approaching.

"Incompetence is the true crisis."
—Albert Einstein,
German-born theoretical physicist

---<>---

Next, get ready to **JUDGE**. Failures and crises offer uncertainties and choices that you can be mindful of. They provide opportunities to decide. However, every decision requires a judgment between choices and consequences.

To judge is the required step towards deciding, experiencing, and exercising your talent as a sculptor.

CHAPTER TWENTY-FIVE:

JUDGE, BABY, JUDGE

Without judgement, you cannot be mindful!

The mindful are curious, aware and attentive; They judge without being judgmental.

Mindfulness accentuates your authenticity. It allows you to judge and be judged, to attach and detach with perspective and awareness. To be mindful is to be brave enough to form an opinion and be paranoid enough to question it. It is to be prepared to attach and detach from ideas, circumstances and choices, over and over. Mindfulness provides you with the freedom to be resilient, but not stubborn. To be flexible, but not indecisive. To remain vulnerable, but not fragile! It provides you with the courage to judge and be judged in order to evolve.

"The eye sees only what the mind is prepared to comprehend."
—Henri Bergson, French philosopher

When I was fourteen, my math teacher forced my parents to have my eyes checked. As a teenager, I was outraged and pushed back, before I eventually gave in. A few weeks later, one summer evening, my father sent me to the optometrist to pick up my glasses. As I stepped out of the store with the new glasses on, I looked at the moon. I was astonished and upset. The moon did not look round anymore. It looked crooked! I was unable to convince the store owner that my prescription was wrong. The next day, I forced my parents to have my eyes checked again by a more competent doctor! The outcome was the same, with the same prescription! I soon realized that it was my judgment and my perception that were crooked. The perfect full moon looked nothing like what I was used to! The moon was always round, but my perception of a perfect circle was biased. To be judgment free is to ignore reality. To assume you have no bias is to ignore human nature. It is to make choices that are confined to the limitation of how we have always seen the world. It is to risk seeing the lunar warped and never knowing the beauty of a real full moon!

To judge is good.
To be judgmental is dangerous.

To be judgmental is to reduce or alter your choices against a filter of your biases. To judge is to discover and eliminate your biases. To be judgmental is to make your biases the driver of your decisions. Misguided judgments lead to bad choices and worse consequences. Our cognitive biases can easily cloud our judgment and taint our awareness. Judge by overemphasizing some pieces of information or accepting facts because they confirm or serve your positions and you compromise your decisions. Aim to find a safe haven in consensus, be overly optimistic, or take mental short cuts by flipping back to an old solution and you compromise your choices. Be an inflexible company founder (suffer from what I call "founderist disease") and limit your future by the limits of your past knowledge and old perspectives. When you let your deliberate or unconscious biases chain your talents and contain your mindfulness, you are impacting your choices and your future.

"The question is not what you look at,
but what you see."
—Henry David Thoreau, American naturalist,
essayist, poet, and philosopher

You will be judged, allow it.

At all times, others perceive and judge you. When you are faced with this judgment, you use your "looking glass of self," your reflection of how you think you appear to others, in order to respond and alter your behavior. You then depend on your imagination on how others feel or what their "real" impressions of you are. You are, therefore, constantly engaging with your formed perception of yourself. The looking glass of self is the window you have into your own mindset as you verify your fears, morality, courage, or bravery. This is how your values and actions are influenced by how others judge you. It is not their judgment that influences your sculpture, but your perception of their judgment.

If you feel judged, first, look within. Your perceptions are influenced by your biases!

The world is connected and your choices, judgments, and decisions are intertwined with others. Be mindful and aware of your judgments. Also, be mindful and aware of your perceptions of their judgments. Actuated mindfulness is about learning and applying. It is more than listening to your inner voice in a vacuum. When mindful, you are open to listen to the "Upaguru," the teacher that is next to you at this moment. Your Upaguru may be a friend at one minute and your kids the next. It could be your customers, your investors, or your employees. It could be Mother Nature or a bumper sticker on the back of a soccer mom's car.

The mindful don't aim to fit things into a certain box in order to understand and act. Relax your creed and change your view. Constantly change your frame of reference and expand your awareness. Compare and judge not from one perspective but from many; that is the path to innovation as well. Look for new insight, discover new value, and innovate. Your biases are both a friend and enemy of innovation. Innovation is often veiled by ambiguity. To unveil it, you must mindfully judge. Because every innovation begins with judgment. Is this good enough? Do I or my customers deserve more? Innovation begins with comparing situations, values, and outcomes. If you are chained by your biases, you compromise your ability to innovate. Discover your predispositions and you have discovered a window to innovation. Every evolution is rooted in comparison of choices. Every sculptor makes choices in order to create.

Be a critical thinker. Critical thinking is the *objective* analysis and evaluation of an issue to form a *judgment* and make a reasonable choice. The key influencing factors are how to decide what is "objective," and what framework will guide your "judgment." To be mindful is to be a critical thinker. As a critical thinker, you are expected to transfer knowledge from one situation to the next. You should be discriminatingly logical and able to break a whole into parts to discover their nature, function, and relationships. You are expected to judge; be data-driven, always curious, and skeptical. You should be able to sense the future, predict, and envision a plan and its consequences. As a sculptor and a practicing entrepreneur, you are a critical thinker who constantly blends experience, intuition, and analytics. You remain mindful of uncertain situations that surround you. In the promising messy life you live in, you must judge conditions and choices and dispute your judgments to improve your probability of success.

Be aware of temptations you can't resist. Look for and control the noise in your perceptions and insight. Be simultaneously a conservative and a liberal. You are a liberal as you remain "open to new behaviors or opinions and willing to discard traditional values." Be a conservative as you "hold on and defend your proven and former attitudes and values." When mindful, you have an evolving PEP that considers new ideas as you seek to shape your new self while preserving the values that make you authentic and effective. You are mindful when you embrace your values, but are open to judge and evolve with them. Like a mindful artist, let yourself judge and be judged.

> *"The painter has the Universe*
> *in his mind and hands."*
> **—Leonardo da Vinci, Italian painter, draftsman,**
> **sculptor, architect, and engineer**

---<>---

Finally, be a sculptor, a **MINDFUL ARTIST**, who stands ready to create an ever-evolving sculpture.

The sculpture of self that is solid, permanent, resilient, but always evolving. A soulful structure built on the foundation of your PEP. A sculpture of you that is purposefully never complete and realistically never perfect.

Next, a last reminder. Don't be clever and aim to change the world first. Be wise and change yourself mindfully over and over.

---<>---

CHAPTER TWENTY-SIX:

THE MINDFUL ARTIST

An entrepreneur, a sculptor, enjoys a transformational mindset. Be ready to embrace the beauty of the unknown and the love of your wisdom. Be always aware and ready to go. Be ready to evolve. As an artist, you appreciate a perspective of life that goes beyond pure logic, one that is not limited by intellect or tainted by your origins. A viewpoint that blends intuition and intellect.

"We should not pretend to understand the world only by the intellect.
The judgment of the intellect is only part of the truth."
—Carl Jung, Swiss psychiatrist and psychoanalyst, father of analytical psychology

We step into a new river every time; an apple thrown up turns 1,000 times. You are never able to predict the exact turn of events in business and life. Life is messy, but within its messiness, creativity, choices, and accomplishments are hidden. A mess that can only be navigated with a transformational mindset.

Art is the domain of the uncertain and unrevealed. The domain of unborn originality. The yin and yang of mindfulness is the duality that must be harmonized. The science of reality and possibilities that must be balanced with the art of imagination, creativity, and determination. Strive to explore both the art and the science of mindfulness with a transformational mindset. Provoke yourself and evoke. Rise up as an artist, acknowledge your entrepreneurial talent and qualities, and pursue your love of wisdom. The world is exposed one event at a time and one change at a time. An artist invents by each stroke of the brush, a sculptor by the impressions of the chisel.

Your sculpture is shaped with every choice YOU make, every action YOU take, and every consequence YOU face.

"Yesterday I was clever, so I wanted to change the world.
Today I am wise, so I am changing myself."
—Jalâluddîn Rumi, 13th century poet
and metaphysicist

---<>---

It is time. Be a conscious author. **IT IS DAY ONE**.

Become the author of your next best chapter. Turn the page and change because choices only come when change is present.

Be you, an authentic leader who situationally explores the axiom of choices in sight. Be an original, regardless of your origins. Acknowledge that the road ahead is jagged and uncertain. Then, purposefully ignite your wanderlust and stand to learn through the wounds of failure. Always remember, you are not them, and pursue your love of wisdom; your Personal Entrepreneurial Philosophy (PEP). The philosophy that will guide your journey.

Judge and choose without judgment. Pursue happiness and stay eager to exchange. Actuate your mindfulness and, as a born entrepreneur, exchange your past and your experiences, your resources, with something better, knowing that you are fully ready and capable of facing the uncertain and messy life we all live in.

Acknowledge that in your life's journey you will never have a full and complete map of your future. In an entrepreneurial journey you are always discovering new frontiers. Don't expect a full and detailed itinerary of your trip before you start. Your path is only constructed when you travel it. Recognize that you can and will always add new colors to your pure talent and choose where you are in the galaxy of entrepreneurship. Observing and reading about the journeys of other entrepreneurs may be interesting and educational, but their journeys belong to them. You are not them! They have constructed and travelled their unique path and you must find and travel yours.

Color your entrepreneurial talent. Stay nervous and embrace crisis. Be a pilot and navigate the perils. Explore your Oceanness and energize, provide, and connect. Dance always. Shift and travel through time, forms, and perspectives and live both in today and tomorrow.

It is the first light, always. It is the first break of day one, always.

Be **THE SCULPTOR AND THE SCULPTURE**! Chisel away! Start writing your chapter...

---<>---

<<END OF PART FOUR>>

PART FIVE:
THE BEGINNING

Next,
the page is blank,
an unwritten letter.

----

*It is a new chapter,
you are the authority,
and the author.*

----

*You are the sculptor
and the sculpture.*

CHAPTER TWENTY-SEVEN:

IT IS DAY ONE

> It is day one, every day.
> It is the beginning, with every choice.
> Start authoring ...

_____

_____

_____

_____

_____

_____

_____

_____

_____

_____

WITH ENDLESS THANKS ...

Fay N. Aleagha
Evelyn Block
Steve Block
Shekhar Chitnis
Avijit Datta
Massoud Ghaemi
Lin Giralt
Ramin Heydari
Farzin Khalkhali
Koz Khosravani
Rajat Khurana
Kathleen Moore
Diako Pahlevan
Reza Pahlevan
Marjan Pirouz
Arsames Qajar
Maryam Shah Hosseini
Michael Trimble
Michael Utvich
&
My True North, My Wife Assal

READY TO UNLEASH YOUR CREATIVITY AND EVOLVE?

Join us for a talk with the author - "YOU ARE NOT THEM!: Meet the Author and Meet Yourself

YOU ARE NOT THEM

THE AUTHENTIC ENTREPRENEUR'S WAY

SID MOHASSEB

Learn more at www.youarenotthem.com/talk.

Made in the USA
Coppell, TX
25 October 2021

64610645R00128